GOD'S HAND

IN THE LIFE
OF AN ELECTRICIAN

GOD'S HAND

IN THE LIFE
OF AN ELECTRICIAN

Jimmy Yamada, Jr.

WHITE
MOUNTAIN
CASTLE
PUBLISHING, LLC

www.whitemountaincastle.com
Kapolei, Hawai'i

God's Hand
in the Life of an Electrician

Copyright © 2008 by Jimmy Yamada, Jr.
Published by White Mountain Castle Publishing, LLC
First Printing, 2008
Second Printing & Third Printing, 2009

We want to hear from you.
Please send your comments or inquiries to:

White Mountain Castle Publishing, LLC
P.O. Box 700833
Kapolei, Hawai'i 96709
Phone: 808 689-3269
Email: whitemountaincastle@yahoo.com
Website: whitemountaincastle.com

Edited by Dawn O'Brien
Cover Design & Text Formatting by Sherrie Dodo
Back Cover Photo by Marc Schechter

ISBN 978-0-9815219-2-3
Printed in Korea

This book is dedicated to Mom and Dad.
I would not be here without them.
Their love, devotion to family, work ethic,
and undying sacrifice for me
(without criticism or complaint!),
built a solid foundation for all that I am today.

I know God was involved in our lives, but still I say:
Thank you Mom! Thank you Dad!
(I know you're in heaven today helping Jesus
build the Yamada house.)

I love you both more than I can express.

Table of Contents

Foreword

Someone once said, "*God's man following God's plan will also see God's hand*."

There is a Bible verse that helps to explain:

> "*If my people, who are called by my name, will humble themselves and pray and seek my face and turn from their wicked ways, then will I hear from heaven and will forgive their sin and will heal their land.*" (2 CHRONICLES 7:14)

God's man: "*If my people, who are called by my name….*" God specifically tells us whom He is talking about – you and I – as we are called by His name.

God's plan: "*…will humble themselves and pray and seek my face and turn from their wicked ways….*" God's plan is that we will humble ourselves, pray always, seek Him, and turn from our wicked ways, which we all have due to our sinful nature.

God's hand: For me the key to humbling myself was realizing what Isaiah discovered long ago: "*Lord… all that we have accomplished, you have done for us*" (ISAIAH 26:12). Anything that I have accomplished with any lasting, eternal value was thanks to the hand of God. All of the supernatural events in my life were of *His* glory: my wife, Diana; my kids, Jason, Daven, and Lisa; my new daughters Donna and Charity; my business; friends and ministry. He had His hand on every aspect of these miracles, whether it was His upraised or His loving hand.

How many Christians can honestly say they sincerely seek the face of God?

My prayer life: What worked for me was prayer scattered throughout the day. I focused less on asking for things as I recognized God's blessings. This is not to imply that I'm so holy that I didn't pray for my needs; I did and He answered. Prayer was simply a way to get me to change from the way I was to the way He wanted me to be. My prayers: *What do you want me to do, Lord? How do you want me to do it? And when?*

As I read the Bible, one of the most intriguing passages was also one of the most confusing: *"If you are pleased with me, teach me your ways so I may **know you** and continue to find favor with you"* (EXODUS 33:13, emphasis added). Then I found another one that helped to clear it up: *"He made known **his ways** to Moses, his deeds to the people of Israel"* (PSALM 103:7, emphasis added). What God meant by *"his ways,"* was reading and understanding the Bible. I began reading it daily and thought about how I could please Him more by living what I read.

The words of Geoff Moore's song "Erase" says it all:

> "Erase all that's different between us
> Until nothing ever separates us
> And we love like You love
> And we ache when You ache
> And our heart is undone
> By what makes Your heart break."

Once we become God's man following God's plan, then He will hear us, forgive us, and ultimately heal our land. God will show up supernaturally in our physical realm. We will hear His voice and see His hand active in our lives – guiding, encouraging, disciplining, and loving us. As God heals our land, we'll see signs and wonders become all too real and very obvious.

Allow me to stress that we should *not* be seeking after miracles and the supernatural. Instead, they should be a natural outcome of drawing closer to Him. Only *then* will we have joy in hearing His voice, just as John the Baptist heard it at Jesus' baptism (MATTHEW 3:13-17). We will have joy in seeing Him involved in simple things – like providing parking, helping us quit drinking or smoking, bringing us a mate – to list a few.

This book is about how I have seen God's hand and His impact on my life. My purpose in writing this book is to glorify God. I give Him credit for all of my successes and I alone take credit for all of my failures. He prospered me in more ways than I can list. I am involved in a variety of ministries and He has used me to help many. I have deliberately refrained from recounting those circumstances where money was involved except for a few instances where I felt that the details were directly relevant.

I apologize for anything written that even remotely draws attention away from Him and towards me. It is not my purpose and although I have been very careful, I'm sure it's there.

1

Growing Up

My earliest recollection of God is of someone who bails you out if you are in trouble.

I never really believed in a God who created the universe. Why should I? I had seen the movie "Fantasia" with its splendid evolutionary sequence. Essentially I was brainwashed into believing that we had evolved from nothing. What impacted me as a young child stayed with me. I didn't know why I believed what I believed. Like osmosis, my soul absorbed all kinds of things. I later realized I had preconceived ideas about race, religion, education, culture, sex... all of it good *and* bad.

Although I didn't believed in a God who interacted with us, I remember praying regularly to Him in two situations. In the fourth grade, I took a pack of cigarettes under our house and smoked one. It was terrible. However, it was heaven compared to what followed.

When I got home, my dad immediately knew I had done something. He called me over to where he was sitting, grabbed my hand, and said, "Blow out." That was it. He then lit a cigarette and gave me a "*yaito.*" In English, he put his cigarette out on my left hand.

When I look at my hand now, it doesn't bear a scar, so he didn't put it out completely on my hand. However, when you're nine years old, this creates a very memorable moment. Thereafter, whenever I did anything wrong, I would pray that my dad wouldn't find out.

My "Good Luck" Prayer

The second situation involved old propeller airplanes. When I was about four years old, my younger brother Ronnie and I would visit our Aunty Helene and Uncle Take and their family on Kaua'i. We spent the next six summers in Kaua'i, and I remember the swimming, camping, fishing, hiking, and *furo* baths (Japanese hot tub) for which we made our own fire. This was heaven for a firebug: making a fire without parental supervision.

The only thing I disliked about those summer visits was the airplane takeoff and landing. Prayer kept me sane. I would rest my right index finger on the bridge of my nose. Then I would pray a "good luck" prayer. Even though I didn't know to whom I was praying, it never let me down and my plane never crashed.

A True Atheist

By the time I entered high school, the media had done its trick. I was a solid atheist – except during airplane rides.

Despite everything, I was a pretty good guy. I was part of two clubs at the Young Men's Christian Association (YMCA): the Impalas (Intermediate) and the Safaris (High School). There were about 14 guys in our gang and we would have died for each other.

Our leader, Mike "Mikel" K. would call and say: "Game on Saturday, 10:30 am, Kawananakoa Field," and everyone showed up: Lloyd "Fuj" F., Paul "Tomo" T., Lorrin "Kuni" K., Ben F., Larry "Moe" U., Myles K., Carl "Mac" M., Melvin "Taka" T., Gary "Grapes" K., Keith "Toejams" O., Dexter "Dex" Tom, and Alvin "DoonGie" Y.

Although we were a Christian club, we weren't there for God. We were there for the sports and the girls! The girls loved us... or so we dreamed! We played football, basketball, and baseball. Most of us were Asian, so we weren't big, but we were quick and talented. In high school, I had a girlfriend, Diana, and my love for her kept me in good standing with the law. While some of our gang cut school and got involved in various degrees of mischief like dabbling in alcohol and marijuana, I stayed straight. They needed a driver and I was happy to accommodate.

My Lifelong Love ~ Diana

No story about my life would be complete without the love of my life, Diana Enokawa. I first remember seeing her picture in the Central Intermediate School newspaper. They had a "Hoss Election," which included categories like "Most Likely to Succeed," "Best Athlete," "Most Outstanding," "Best Looking," and Diana was "Most Cutest."

I thought she was the best-looking girl I had ever seen. Her smile reached down into my soul and imprinted itself in my mind. Usually, those crushes don't count for much as you move on with reality, plus there was no way a guy like me stood a chance with "Miss Cutest."

However, my most immediate problem was that Diana was literally out of my reach: a different school district!

Can God Move the School District Line?

I believe we can only see God's invisible hand upon our lives when He gives us revelation. He has to help us to see clearly. Which is why what He gives to one person may not be clear to another. My favorite example of this is how he brought Diana to Roosevelt High School so I could claim her.

Diana's family, the Enokawas, was a large family. The oldest is Doris, followed by Janice, Marvin, Diana, Wilfred, Elaine, and Sterling ("Junki"), the baby. They grew up in a slum of Honolulu called Buckle Lane. Eventually they moved to School Street just north of the Nu'uanu YMCA. Since Doris was the eldest child she was the mother figure of the family as Ma and Pa Enokawa were never home.

The three oldest Enokawa kids went to McKinley High School, but just when Diana finished middle school, the district was realigned. Off she went to Roosevelt High. (Oddly enough, the next year, when her younger brother Wilfred was set to go to high school, the district realigned again. In fact, Elaine and Junki also went to McKinley High, which meant only Diana attended Roosevelt.) When I look back, I can see God's hand. He moved the district line twice: Once to get Diana into Roosevelt and then a second time to help me realize that He can move the school district line at will.

When I look back, I can see God's hand.

Back to Diana

At Central Intermediate School, Diana was part of a group of girls that were called the "Les Charmaines." They were, as their name indicates, the "Best of the Best." They were beautiful, outspoken, class leaders, and brainy. They were just too popular. All the boys were after them.

But when Diana was sent to Roosevelt High School without the "Charmaines," she was like a duck out of water. She had virtually no friends and was, therefore, vulnerable to my "attack." I believe God orchestrated the whole scenario.

Eventually she became "my girl" and I was the happiest guy at Roosevelt High. We were together all through college. I would pick her up for school in my hot rod, a '57 Chevy, and life was great. One of the neatest things about Diana was she liked what I liked. I liked football (San Francisco 49ers and University of Hawai'i), bridge (she became a great partner), poker with the gang (she was the cook, the host, and the clean-up), and surfing (she would come and wait on the beach). There was nothing better than coming in from a three-hour surf session to see your girlfriend waving from the beach.

Life Gets Better...in College

I did well all through college at the University of Hawai'i (UH), except for playing pool in Hemenway Hall and bridge in Keller Hall. We also surfed a lot. I was sure life couldn't get any better. Little did I know how close I was to being right.

In the beginning of my senior year (1968), Mikel (who was attending the University of Washington) was home and took a bunch of us to a Waikiki bar. I had my first Seven-Seven: a mix of Seven-Up and Seagram's Seven. I got bombed and it was a blast.

Life changed that night. And so began the second phase of my life: alcohol and drugs, nightclubs and loose living. Of course, at the time, it all seemed normal.

High Society & Fast Times

Once I had a taste of the life I had been "missing," I made up for lost time in a hurry. Prior to the summer of '68, I thought I would graduate with a degree in electrical engineering from UH, get a job, and marry Diana. But alcohol changed me.

One night we were out at a pizza parlor and I met another woman. Within four months, I was dating both girls. "Your ultimate test," said Diana, "will be who you take out on Christmas Eve." Well, it wasn't her.

We broke up and I started dating yet another girl. After three years, we eventually broke up. My partying was in high gear and my drinking menu featured Primo beer, Crown Royal, Galliano, Southern Comfort, Courvoisier, to name a few. We also tried different kinds of wines, envisioning ourselves as high society.

I was also smoking *pakalolo* (marijuana) and hashish (marijuana sap). The *pakalolo* was so good that after we rolled our cigarette joints our fingers were sticky from the resin. One hit and you reached your destination. Of course, we kept traveling.

We convinced ourselves that we were only doing the "safe" stuff because we didn't do heroin, acid, or LSD. I purchased a house in Moanalua Valley and we called it "Moanalua Gang's Palace." We were the kings of the valley.

Though I didn't have a personal relationship with Jesus, I knew God was watching over me. Each weekend was "party time," We would go to the clubs or different house parties and I was always looking for a girl. One day, I was sitting at home pondering my life and trying to figure out what I was looking for and I had a revelation: I was looking for a girl that looked and acted like Diana. She was a remarkable woman.

Though I didn't have a personal relationship with Jesus, I knew God was watching over me.

Although Diana was hurt for being abandoned, she never showed it and never spoke badly about me.

We had stayed on friendly terms, so I gathered the courage to call her up. Despite of her engagement to another guy (with the wedding just a few short months away!), I told her I wanted her back. She agreed, broke off her engagement, and moved in with me. (Remember, we were not Christians.)

About a year later, on October 27, 1973, we were married. However, my drinking and partying habits were solidly entrenched. On my wedding night, my gang came over to "Moanalua Gang's Palace" to continue the party. However, I was so drunk, I crashed as soon as I got home. Diana, being the angel she was (and still is), never said a thing the next day. I know most wives today would have been ready to ring hell's bells.

Brush with Bankruptcy

After I got married, I went to work for my dad, James Takashi Yamada. He was an astute businessman and spent 20 years building his company, A-1 A-Lectrician (A-1).

A-1 went through a disastrous period from 1976 through 1978. I almost single-handedly bankrupted us. We had taken on two large projects – Century Center and Makiki Park Place. I had negotiated and managed both projects, and in two years lost most of the net worth of A-1. My dad had accumulated a nice sum of cash outside of the business. He was forced to sell all of his assets and invest the money back into the business.

At the same time, I sold Moanalua Gang's Palace and invested the proceeds into our business. It was to be the single best financial investment I have ever made. And to this day, I've kept the name "Junior" so people remember that A-1 had a founder, my father.

Back on Top

Our business recovered by 1981 as we did many of the high rises in downtown Honolulu. Our projects included Honolulu Tower, Nuʻuanu Craigside, Hale Kaheka, and Century Square. The one thing that didn't change was my addiction. I was an alcoholic. Of course, at that time I was sure I was *not* an alcoholic. In 1980, I even set out to prove it…I had to for my peace of mind: I quit drinking for one whole year. At the end of the year I was so proud of myself. I had proven that I wasn't an alcoholic. What did I do the next day? I got bombed. Wine was my new drink. Red, white, rose and champagne – I didn't discriminate. Oh, how I had reached greater heights of class!

Angel in a Car Crash

In August of 1981, I was out with a good contractor friend. We had gone to Horatio's and ended up at a famous bar, Club Rose (infamous for its decadence). I headed home after possibly 10 drinks (only God knows), and as I was driving around Kamehameha Highway near Makalapa Gate – I had missed the H1 on-ramp – the mountain attacked me and gave me a judo throw for an *ippon* (knockout).

When I came to my car was upside-down. Its roof was completely flattened. I should have died or at the very least broken my neck or my back. Instead Diana came to pick me up while I waited in the guard station. While sitting there, I remember her walking up the highway, five months pregnant, holding our oldest son Jason's hand.

The next day, she took me to look at my car, which was totaled. I don't recall asking her how she felt; I didn't want to know. As I looked at the car, I remember thinking how lucky I was. As I look back today, I believe an angel from God saved me that night.

A Wake-Up Call

Our business recovered from another tough period in the mid-'80s when I had to lay off half of our workforce. Things turned around in 1987 and it was a good year. By this time, I was sure God was not real, at least not in the way that the "crazy Christians" portrayed Him. In September, I had an epiphany.

Our kids were involved in various sports. Our boys were in judo and soccer. Judo was Monday, Wednesday, and Friday from 5 pm to 8 pm. Tuesdays and Thursdays were for soccer practices. They did their homework on the fly and we ate dinner on the run. On Saturday, judo was from 8 am to noon… unless they had soccer, in which case we left judo to go to the soccer game.

When Jason and Daven got into soccer, I volunteered to be a referee. You are either a soccer ref that everyone respects and loves to see in the game, or one that everyone hates on game day, in which case "boos" and complaints greet your calls. My first year was tough; I received many snide sideline remarks. I vowed that my second year would be better. I went to referee classes, read the soccer manual, and watched games. I kept my vow and became a good referee; at least my family didn't have to cover their heads with a paper bag after the game.

All was fine until Jason reached the 12-13 age bracket. I arrived on the first day of practice and fear struck. *There is no way I will be able to keep up with these kids!*

We changed from a system of having just one referee and two linesmen to a two-referee system. I needed more speed to keep up and I just didn't have it. I adjusted reasonably well until "Black Saturday." It followed a Friday night party when I had had eight beers. The game was early the next morning. It was horrible.

Normally you referee the game *after* the game your kids play in. Or, if their team plays the last game, then you referee the first game of the day. I don't recall the reason, but I was refereeing our kids' own game.

On the worst call of the game, the coach's son purposely attacked and tripped his opponent who was racing for the goal on a breakaway. I was 20 yards behind and had a bad angle, so I couldn't see the play to make the call. However, the foul was so blatant that the coach stopped the play and pulled his son out of the game. He saved my life, but not my pride: I deserved to be crucified for not being in position to make the call. If I didn't have that hangover, I would have made it. And it wasn't the only bad call. I hung my head as I walked my family to the car.

"Freedom Day": Quit or Die!

The following Monday, my 20-month old daughter Lisa was trying to play with me. I had just come home from work and was lying on our living room floor, trying to rest from a hard day's work and a hard night before. Lisa was crawling on my back, saying, "Daddy, play with me!" I was too tired to move. Although my body was dead, I had an epiphany: *You're a jerk and a bum! You can't even play with your daughter, much less keep up with adolescent kids.*

The next day was "Freedom Day." As I drove to work, I thought of the soccer game and how I embarrassed myself and my family. To make it worse, I kept hearing Lisa's little voice saying, "Daddy, play with me!" Something rose up in my soul.

So many times when I awoke with a hangover, I would say to myself, *One day I'm going to quit drinking.* This was the day. I shouted at the top of my lungs, with passion (as if my beloved 49ers had just won a playoff game), "I quit drinking!"

A few weeks later I celebrated my *yakudoshi* (fortieth birthday) clean and sober. I have never taken a drink since.

Is There a God?

In the late '80s, I met regularly with a very good contractor friend who shared with me evidence for the existence of God. We would get together for lunch two or three times a year, and each time he would present something new. After five years of this, I went from a 99 percent atheist to an 80 percent atheist.

In late '92, Kevin Asano (1988 Olympics silver medalist in judo) gave me a book by Josh McDowell, *Evidence that Demands a Verdict.* After reading it, I moved from an 80 percent atheist to a believer. I remember coming to that place of sweet revelation: "THERE IS A GOD!"

In late May I had lunch with another friend, Sam Nonaka, and talked about the importance of leaving our kids with good values and a strong character. It was something I was proud of doing with my own children...or so I thought. He made a statement that stuck with me: "If you leave your kids with the knowledge of God, He will always be there to guide them and to help them."

> *"If you leave your kids with the knowledge of God He will always be there to guide them and to help them"*

Later that week, I asked Diana what she thought about going to church, expecting a negative response. But as my precious Diana has done over the years, she surprised me. "I think that would be good for the kids!" she sweetly said.

So Diana, Lisa, and I went to First Assembly of God on June 6, 1993. At the end, Pastor Sapp asked if anyone wanted to receive Jesus as Lord and Savior. After his prayer, when everyone's eyes were closed and heads were bowed, Diana looked up to the front of the sanctuary. "Look," she told Lisa, "Dad's up there!"

My life changed forever.

2

About My Father's Business

There is nothing like success in business to double the size of one's head. When I first joined A-1, my dad made me vice president, which didn't mean much since he ran the company. My father's way of managing was from the old school: If I stuck my neck out and grabbed responsibility, and set up something that worked, I could continue having responsibility for that task. Little by little he allowed me to run more of the business.

One day in the early '70s, a Porsche 914 caught my eye. Everyone knows that a young business executive cannot develop new business without a hot car. Gathering all of my courage, I went into dad's office and asked if I could get that car. He asked me about the car and how much it would cost. After I told him, his response increased the size of my head another 50 percent: "Well, you're the vice president!" This was the start of my downfall. I didn't have the Book's wisdom, which warns: "Pride comes before the fall."

Big Business, Bigger Attitude

Pride blinded me to the limitations we had as a company. In early '73, as Diana and I strolled hand-in-hand down Kalakaua Avenue, we stopped and I craved after what I saw. Hyatt Regency Waikiki was being constructed: two large towers were coming out of the ground and I said to myself: "That's what I want to build." Three years later we were working on what was to become our company's largest project ever: Century Center.

It was to give me the greatest life lesson. But until my graduate-level lesson kicked in, my head grew another 50 percent. I thought I was God's gift to the Yamadas and to Diana.

My drinking and marijuana habit aside, my biggest blind spot was not recognizing the amazing gift that God had given me, Diana. I did what many business executives did: work hard at the office and cruise at home. I also let my enlarged head (it was hard to fit through my front door) start to change my attitude towards my wife.

Since I was the boss at work, I had everything done my way. It wasn't long before that came home too. My sharp tongue cut at her with criticism and complaint. I thought I was right 100 percent of the time. I became terribly impatient and domineering.

If we had a dinner business date, I would remind Diana the night before that dinner was at 7 pm and we would need to leave by 6 pm. I would remind her again that morning and again a couple of hours before. By 6 pm, if she wasn't ready, I would announce to the world that I was going to wait in the car, and would patiently wait until 6:05 pm. Then I would lovingly pop my horn for about 2 seconds, in case she didn't know I was waiting.

Baby Monster

If we ran out of soap at home, I would ask: "How come we don't have soap?" My comments were spoken with a tinge of aggravation about whatever the shortage was at the time. But my pride created a bigger problem: a baby monster.

Eventually my conscience would convict me and I wished I didn't complain or criticize. However, I couldn't seem to stop! My responses seemed built-in to my DNA. I would consciously make a mental note not to react critically. I even promised myself that I wouldn't blast my horn while waiting for her. These mental programs worked for a while, but never had any lasting impact.

I wondered why I couldn't love my wonderful wife in this area; she was the most important person in my life! I even reflected on our early courting, when I viewed her as my queen. This became an area of considerable frustration for me. Each time I reacted negatively, my stock in myself headed south. This struggle continued from shortly after our marriage until my conversion to Christ in June 1993.

Returning to My First Love

The first pledge I made after coming to Christ was to love Diana the way I had loved her in the early days. The Bible commands husbands to love their wives as Christ loves the church. That was something I dearly desired. One might say it was an "impossible dream" – it had been my struggle for so long! – but that was my desire. And for the first time in decades, I gained a victory: I stopped criticizing and horn-popping!

> *The Bible commands husbands to love their wives as Christ loves the church.*

The first real test came in Thanksgiving 1993. Diana was going to Sunny Side Bakery in Wahiawa and I offered to drive. "You're so lucky to have me drive," I commented magnanimously, "you get to sit back and enjoy the scenery!" I was fishing for a loving response with "respect" in its mouth. Instead she joked, "Ugh! So humbug!" It hurt. Yet I resolved not to let the "Empire Strike Back." I was quiet the rest of the way.

When I got home, I saw dishes in the sink. *No way!* I said to myself. However, I knew I should go ahead and do them. As an act of love I proceeded to do something I *never* would have done before I became a Christian.

The Impossible Dream Comes True!

That first year after my conversion, I had more patience and love for my wife. That was huge for me as it showed that God was real and could help me accomplish the impossible. He answered my prayer: "Father, help me to love Diana like you love her." My faith grew on this seemingly small change.

In the early Christian years, loving Diana came relatively easy. Meanwhile, she had actually been conditioned by our first 20 years of marriage – where I had been a samurai with a quick-and-sharp sword and she had to be the perfect wife. This wonderful woman had taken all of the years of criticizing and complaining in stride.

Then, about the fourth year, something happened. Diana realized she didn't have to be so accommodating: Her samurai no longer had a sword! Instead, he was like a gentle farmer. So she too changed; Diana was able to allow her true self to blossom. She could make comments that in previous years might have caused me to draw my sword (verbally, of course). She no longer had to worry or tweak her reactions. Two incidents shed light on how she was changing, too.

Saving Her Spot

One day we were reading the paper and I made a few comments about the articles. She slammed her paper down and said, "You don't have to tell me what's happening! I read the paper from the beginning to end and I read *every* article." Then she picked up her paper and continued reading. Boy that hurt! Without reacting, I stood up, went to my room and prayed: "God, help heal this pain in my heart."

The next day was Saturday and we usually went to 24 Hour Fitness together to workout. Since I had an early men's meeting, I arrived before she did and wondered whether I should save her spot as I normally did. I paused, and then turned into the room, put down her step climber, and put a CD on it to hold her spot.

When she arrived, I was stretching with my head to the mat. She put her hand on my shoulder and said, "You're an angel! I know you were upset last night, but you still saved me a spot." My soul was fed.

Appreciating the "Small Things"

The second incident involved a young man named Jonathan. Our son Daven had a band called "The Epic Sessions." Jonathan was 17 years old, his mother was living on the mainland and he was living with his father who also was moving to the mainland. Because he was a minor he couldn't live by himself, so Daven asked if Jonathan could live with us. It was only for four months until he became 18.

Diana was not excited. Her workload in our home would increase. She was already making lunches for five. "Well," I said, "you'll just have to add Jonathan to the list." Diana has a wonderful gift of serving, so what I had said was foolish and unnecessary.

She replied, "I do love making lunch for Jason (our eldest son). He always lets me know how much he appreciates me."

That hurt. I thought, *What about me?*

Men are dysfunctional. We are easily hurt, especially by our wives. Yet God knew that at the same time we desperately need respect. So God wisely advised via Paul in the Bible: "*The wife must respect her husband*" (EPHESIANS 5:33).

That night I hurt badly. I went to my room and immediately started thinking about all the things I did to show my appreciation for her. In fact, I was convinced that I should have made her "Top Two" list of people who most appreciated her!

I tried reading my Bible but nothing registered. After an hour of turmoil, I went to bed, but of course I couldn't fall asleep. After another hour I finally felt my eyes getting heavy, so I prayed the holiest prayer I could muster: "God take me tonight, in Jesus' name."

"Good Morning!"

The next morning I awoke and thought, *What am I going to say when I see her?* After a few seconds, a revelation came: *I'll say, "Good morning!"*

Diana was in the kitchen. I walked in and said, "Good morning!" She responded the same and everything was fine.

The lesson for me was that even though Diana could react in freedom, my reaction was not to be with a sharp sword directed at her, but a prayer towards God the Father. From that night on, when I felt hurt, I prayed in my affliction: "Father, help ease the pain that this woman you gave me brought on me." I would no longer react to Diana but direct my hurt to the God who created us.

> My reaction was not with a sharp sword directed at her but a prayer towards God the Father.

While you may think this is a small thing, it really was huge. Diana has always been a great wife. Yet in the past six years she has truly become a woman after God's own heart. She has drawn closer to God and, in doing so, has become an even better wife. God touched and impacted Diana in a way that I never could.

3

Adding Children to the Mix

If kids lived a perfect life after giving their lives to Jesus, parenting would be bliss. Wouldn't it be wonderful if children obeyed their parents and did *not* argue, did *not* participate in disapproved activities, did *not* date until 25 years of age? Then Christianity would be worth it even if God *was* only a fable. But that's not Biblical and it's certainly not reality – it's Fantasyland.

When Diana and I became Christians in 1993, our children reacted in different ways. The two youngest, Daven and Lisa accepted what we told them about Christianity: we were sinners in need of a Savior and Jesus paid the price for our sins. If we believed in Jesus Christ, we could enter into a relationship with God. Our oldest son Jason (17) thought his dad had "lost his marbles." He kept waiting for me to come to my senses.

I spent a lot of time presenting the Gospel message and shared from Josh McDowell's book, *Evidence that Demands a Verdict.* Eventually Jason understood and believed. (I highly recommend that you read his book. If you bought this book and cannot afford McDowell's book, contact me and I will personally mail you a copy.)

Learning to Love Unconditionally

By that time though, Jason had many bad habits and unholy desires. One day when he was almost 20 years old, we had had enough and were ready to kick him out. I left for a trip and on the plane I read the book of Romans. Then it hit me: We could not legislate Jason's morality; instead, we would have to leave it to God to change his life.

In fact, the very "law" we were using to get him to change his life was actually producing in him "*every kind of covetous desire*" (ROMANS 7:8). Jesus commanded us to love one another unconditionally and that applied to our son too. It became clear that kicking him out, when he presented no danger to the family, would *not* be unconditional love.

> *Jesus commanded us to love one another unconditionally and that applied to our son too.*

So we changed tactics and started to love Jason just as he was. We didn't try to stop him from drinking and clubbing. (Basically he was doing what I had done when I was his age.) It got worse. One day I opened his door and I almost fell over from the alcohol vapors that were thick as Los Angeles' smog.

When he woke up that afternoon, I lovingly sat down with him and gently said, "I know you got loaded last night. I can smell it, so just tell me the truth: How many did you have last night?" It took him a second, but finally Jason said, "About eight drinks." I figured he had more, but I gently told him, "God is going to cut off your legs."

Startled, he looked at me and said, "What?"

I repeated, "God is going to cut off your legs." I hadn't planned what I was going to say, but I believe God gave me these words to prophesy to my son.

A Few Warning Shots

A few months later, Jason was working on the jobsite and got something in his eye. It was a little after 5 pm on Friday and our general foreman, Fongie, called an eye doctor for Jason. Normally the doctor was gone by that time, but he took the appointment since he knew Fongie. The doctor removed a small piece of rusted metal from Jason's eye and told him he was lucky he had come in when he did. If he had waited until the next day, it would have required major eye surgery, as the eye would have started to encapsulate the metal.

A few months after that, Jason rammed the whole right side of his precious Toyota SR5 truck into a five-inch diameter tree just 75 yards from our home. After thinking about the two incidents, and remembering the word I believe God had given me about "cutting off his legs," I called Jason into my home office and sat him down on the bed. This is where serious discussions took place. It was also where the children had their disciplinary "super-*chai*'s" (spankings) when they were young.

"Remember when I told you a few months ago," I said to my son, "that God was going to cut off your legs?" He remembered. Then I laid out for him what I believed God was doing. The eye injury was God showing him that he was "lusting with his eyes." His truck crash was God revealing his craving for possessions. "But, Dad," he interrupted, "a dog ran in front of the truck!" I told him, "Who do you think sent the dog?"

The Final Blow

Then I explained to Jason how God loved him so much that He was revealing what would happen if Jason continued to live a sinful life. And that would be to take the one thing Jason was most proud of: his legs. Jason's legs represented his ability to do all the things he was really good at – surf, judo, and work as an electrician. These were his strengths.

Tears started to flow as Jason fell back on the bed. He lay there for some time, then sat up and wiped his face. "Dad, I got it," he said. Those words were like Beethoven's Ninth Symphony to my ears. I believe Jason heard the Lord and felt His love.

That began Jason's journey to becoming the man of God he is today. Looking back, I see the power in God's *agape*, His unconditional love. The Bible says that sanctification, or becoming more like Jesus, is a slow process and a work of the Holy Spirit. I believe most parents get in the way of the Holy Spirit's work. We don't really believe God will do what He promises to do through the Holy Spirit. So we take control and use the Law as a whipping rod for our adult kids.

> *I believe most parents get in the way of the Holy Spirit's work.*

Imagine what power we can unleash in our kids when we do things God's way!

Daven & Epic Sessions: "God Said What?!"

Our son Daven was part of a band, Epic Session, with a bunch of friends: Josh Yafuso, Josh Garan, and Jonathan Gorman. A few years ago, Daven's church, Grace Bible, had a prophecy seminar in November. It was planned months in advance and Daven was excited to attend.

However, in early September, Daven told us that Epic Sessions had a opportunity for a gig on Johnson Island. It would pay $4,500 plus all expenses; this would be their biggest payday ever. Daven wanted our advice, saying that if he didn't go, the group probably couldn't play. I bit my tongue and asked Daven what he thought God was telling him to do. God has been utilizing wireless communication long before AT&T, and if Daven asked God, He would guide him. Actually, I was certain that God would want Daven to attend the prophetic conference. Daven was considering full-time ministry and the conference was an important part of his church life.

A few weeks went by and Daven finally came and told us he had heard from God. God told him he should go to Guam. I thought, *God said WHAT? Yeah right, Daven!*

Yet I believed that Daven, had to develop his personal relationship with the Father through the Holy Spirit. If he couldn't be obedient in these seemingly simple situations, how could we expect him to make decisions that would impact his whole life?

Off to Johnson Island they went. It was during Thanksgiving so we missed Daven during our family holiday. When he returned we were anxious to see if he had heard from God, though not expecting much. Oh parents of little faith!

Daven shared that there was much free time since he was on the island for a whole week. He spent a lot on time with God among the coral reefs. Then he dropped the bomb: God wanted him to leave Epic Sessions.

After he left the band, he became more active in church, playing the guitar and drums and even leading worship. He graduated from the University of Hawai'i majoring in business with a minor in music. He then went to a Los Angeles to attend a six-month intensive leadership training school for full-time ministry. Today he is leading a small church on the University of Hawai'i campus planted by Innovative Concepts. God knows better than we do.

"Lisa, You Have Gifts from God!"

Our youngest is our daughter Lisa. From a very young age, she excelled in school and I believe a big part of that was her night-time routine. Every night, Lisa would ask, "Mom, sleep with me," and reading became a daily affair. She became an avid reader and flew through a book a week. Lisa read adult books, such as Frank Peretti's *Piercing the Darkness* while she was in intermediate school. Reading impacted other subjects and she was an honor student throughout school.

One day, when Lisa was a fifth grader at Moanalua Elementary School, I picked up a book she was reading. It included monsters, gore, and evil; I felt it was a highly inappropriate. "Where did you get this book?" I asked. She answered, "From my English teacher." Diana and I reviewed the book and decided for a change to a Christian school. We had already been considering the change for her seventh grade, but this moved everything up a year.

Lisa Grows Up Quick

Lisa went to Christian Academy for a year and then Hawai'i Baptist Academy (HBA). When she was in the ninth grade we had an opportunity to start a Bible study for her classmates at our home. We had just finished a "life group" Bible study and thought it would be manageable to have two groups on the same night. Diana drove to the school in the van from our shop and picked up the kids.

It was a busy day but it was worth seeing the youth grow in Christ. Towards the end of the school year, there was an incident. Lisa and her friends were going to a concert on the North Shore. She told us a deceptive story about where they were going afterwards and who would be bringing her home. It was unnecessary – had she told us the truth, we would have allowed her to do it. Yet the deceit was so deliberate that we stopped her Bible study at the end of the school year.

Lisa took it well. We did not rant and rave or accuse her of lying. We did not ground her for the rest of high school. We explained that although she and the other leaders were very creative in moderating the study, her character development was not where it needed to be a leader. One of the great benefits of the study was we got to know her friends well. We will always be, Uncle Jimmy and Aunty Diana to them.

Moving Like Moses - Many Times!

Lisa eventually went to the University of Hawai'i. One day, in her third semester, she shared where God was moving her. I had just used a passage about Moses leading his people out of Egypt. Lisa began with the same passage: "Just as Moses was leading the Jews out of Egypt, I feel God is leading me go to college in California." We thought she was joking and hoped the issue would pass; however, she wasn't and it didn't.

A few weeks later we discussed it and since Lisa actually was serious, we set up ground rules. For us, a strong Christian college was top priority. Lisa wanted something that combined photography and journalism. We eventually found two colleges that met all of our criteria: Loyola Marymount University and Azusa Pacific University (APU). We visited both and Lisa chose APU, was accepted and started in 2005. By October, I received a call from Lisa. She was now majoring in business, but also considering a change.

After she was at APU for only eight months, Lisa told me she wanted to switch to journalism. APU did not have it. She would need to move to Pepperdine University in Southern California. She was apologetic and accepted the idea that her change may have to wait. As I listened, I felt God speak to my heart and tell me, "Isn't this what both of you were praying for all this time?" So I immediately said to Lisa, "Your mom and I have been praying for you to use your gift of writing to change the world. I believe mom and I can help support your move to find God's plan for you."

Although we pointed her gift of writing out to her, we were never controlling. She knew that our love for her was unconditional. We always told her, "Lisa, there is nothing you could do that would cause us to love you less."

Lisa turned in her application and we didn't expect her to be accepted in the middle of the school year, but she was. Three consecutive semesters of 4.0 grade point averages probably helped, but we also believe God's hand was in it.

A neat by-product of being close with your children is that you get to speak into their lives. And, as an added blessing, you get to guide them on a path that you think is God's plan. We saw Jason go into construction and Daven into ministry. Lisa's gift was communicating ideas through writing. All of them are using the gifts that God gave them.

Feasting at Dinner

When I first came to the Lord, we had Bible study every night at dinner. As the kids became adults, we changed this to once a week. We all shared what God was doing in our lives, good or bad. It was a neat way of bringing God into our family time without being so religious. Mom and dad were not preaching and correcting the whole time. The kids loved it. They saw our weaknesses; we accepted them for theirs. Our focus was what God was doing: hearing His voice and seeing His hand in our lives.

4

God Interested in Me?
Why Don't I Believe It?

If all you have is a hammer, everything starts to look like a nail.

Before I became a Christian, nothing in the universe looked like God was involved. After I became a Christian, it became clear that everything was impacted by the hand of God.

When I flipped my car and survived, I thought I was lucky. Only after Christ came into my life did I realize God's hand. You may think I'm overboard in viewing God's impact in these events.

"Give thanks in all circumstances, for this is God's will for you in Christ Jesus" (1 THESSALONIANS 5:18)

I believe I cannot go wrong with giving God credit and thanking him for providing me with everything. Even for parking spots! *"Give thanks in all circumstances, for this is God's will for you in Christ Jesus"* (1 THESSALONIANS 5:18, emphasis added). Whether I find good parking or not doesn't matter; I love him regardless.

Diana and I first realized God's direction just after we started going to church. We noticed that many messages on the Christian radio station and by our own pastor covered similar topics. We wondered if there might be an overall "controller" coordinating these messages. Then it hit us: Was God orchestrating the teachings?

It hit like a lightning bolt: *God can speak to us!*

We now understand that God speaks to us if we desire to hear from Him. If you do not believe that, then unfortunately you'll never see Him or hear from Him. I began to believe and started looking for His hand in all circumstances.

God Uses "The Sway"

When we joined our church, Diana volunteered to work in the nursery. I followed. One of my God-given gifts is my hip-swaying. I loved to dance. I could sway and rock my kids to sleep. My boast was that I could put any baby to sleep within 10 minutes. Diana often had trouble putting our baby Lisa to sleep. She would give Lisa to me and in about 10 minutes, I would "rock" her to sleep. Everything was fine as long as I was home. If I wasn't home, Lisa would cry and cry. Of course, this was great for my ego, except that it became my job.

My talent came in handy in the nursery. One day, a mother brought her little baby Ryan and he was a terror. No one could get him to stop crying; however, "The Sway" tamed the terror. A few months later, the church administrator introduced us to Ryan's mom, Cherry. She told us she had some trouble with her husband, Renato, who was into drugs. Then, weeks later, he came to church and gave his life to Jesus. As one of the counselors, I prayed with him and was responsible for staying in touch with him.

The very next Tuesday, I called Renato and asked, "How are you doing?" In broken English, he answered, "Not too good."

"Have you tried praying?" I asked.

"What good will that do?" he quipped.

My faith was still in its infancy. I thought, *Oh Lord, why did you give me this person?*

Becoming Brothers-in-Spirit

About a month later, Renato overdosed and was at Wahiawa Hospital. I visited and prayed for him. We really connected – I didn't criticize or condemn, but encouraged him to start again.

The next few months were very interesting. Renato wanted to start a new life. To do that he needed to go into the Salvation Army's Adult Rehabilitation Center. However, first he had to clear a bench warrant issued for his arrest. He had cosigned a car loan for an ex-girlfriend who had not kept up with payments. He was subpoenaed for a court appearance, but failed to appear. When I accompanied him to the police station, neither of us knew what to expect. When we checked in, he was told that the bail was $1,000. Renato didn't have it. Right then, God spoke to me: "You do!" So I told the officer, "I'll post the bond." Renato looked at me like a son would to a father in a special moment.

After that I took Renato to his parents' home in Haleiwa on the North Shore. They lived in plantation housing in the mountains above the plains. I never knew it existed. First, we picked-up three bags of groceries for his family. We spent almost the whole day together and I felt a tinge of sadness as I said goodbye. It was like Renato and I had always been brothers.

Bail Jumper?

The weekend before the hearing, I started to wonder, *What if Renato doesn't appear?* After all, he could miss his bus or otherwise be detained. Actually, I admit I was thinking about the $1,000. So I asked Diana if Renato could sleep at our house on Sunday night since the hearing was Monday. That evening we had dinner with the family. Renato thanked us: he had never had dinner at the table with another family before.

The next morning, I drove him to the courthouse on Alakea Street. Cherry met us there. We didn't know what to expect. We found out that the total owed for the car loan was near $10,000. It was extremely disheartening and much too large to even consider paying off. Still, we waited grimly for our turn. When the judge called Renato's name, he and Cherry went up. The judge then called the plaintiff. He did not appear. We didn't understand what was happening, but very quickly the judge said, "Case dismissed!"

That day, Renato and Cherry saw first-hand the favor of God and they were ecstatic. His guiding hand was clear to me too. Renato could begin the next phase of his journey with God.

> His guiding hand was clear to me too.

As a skeptic, you could come up with five logical reasons for the outcome of the case and explain why God had nothing to do with it. (I recommend that you read Josh McDowell's book, *Evidence That Demands a Verdict*.)

The Salvation Army

The Salvation Army was started by William Booth and his wife Catherine. They had left their church because they disagreed with the elders on their church mission. The elders wanted Booth to pastor a church. Instead Booth wanted to reach out to the homeless, the hungry, the poor, and the addicts and have Jesus change their lives. Today they have an army of over two million strong across the world touching people for Jesus.

My friend Renato is one of those lives that was impacted by the Salvation Army. He was accepted into the Salvation Army's Adult Rehabilitation Center (ARC) program in Iwilei, Hawai'i. I felt that God wanted me to visit him so on the Friday of the week he went in, so I went down to see if they accepted visitors. They did, and we sat at a table outside the cantina. We talked about how things were going in the program and then opened the Bible to Psalm 1. The next week I returned and we did Psalm 2. By the third week another one of the men there asked to join us and within two months we had six guys.

A critical juncture took place at the end of the six-month period: Renato graduated. What would I do? I had planned to continue only as long as Renato was in the program, but I could see that there were hungry men sitting with us on Fridays who were coming voluntarily for the Word of God. I sought God's guidance through prayer. I believe His answer was the half dozen men that were sitting there on Renato's final Friday. They knew I had followed him into the program and asked me if I was coming back. God's direction was clear: I was back the next Friday. That was 11 years ago.

"I'm in the Lord's Army!"

The next milestone came two years later in the program. I was still going weekly, every Friday. I knew that God had lead me to start it and since He never said to stop, I simply continued. One day the Captain (the Salvation Army officers are ranked since it is an army at war) called me into his office. He informed me that they had to let go of their chaplain due to financial constraints. He then asked if I wanted to take over. My price was right for them. And to this day I tell the clients that the Army can fire me, but they cannot cut my pay. I took the position and moved the visit day to Tuesdays.

The class was voluntary, but because I brought snacks from the best snack shop in Honolulu, Wholesale Unlimited, we drew between 12 to 15 men regularly. We even used the boardroom with its big table. In the cantina, we were forced to have to join two or three tables together, which may have made William Booth smile.

Teen Challenge: A Gang for God

One Sunday night, I went to church to hear Steve Boston speak about a rehab program called Teen Challenge. At the end of the service, one of my prophetic sisters in Christ, Dora Chua suggested that we consider hosting Teen Challenge. Dora and her husband, Pastor Hock Lin Chua had a profound impact on Diana's and my spiritual growth. Her suggestion was odd but I took it to God in prayer.

That year, Diana and I had wanted to do something different for Thanksgiving. Over the next few weeks, we felt the Lord confirm that He wanted us to host the Teen Challenge group of about 25 young men for Thanksgiving.

The gang from Teen Challenge enjoyed a day of feasting, swimming, diving, basketball, ping-pong, and fellowshipping. It was a treat for them and also for our family to see them enjoy themselves. For just one day we were blessed as these men struggling with addiction, drew closer to Jesus instead.

"Going for Broke" for God

The very next week I felt the Lord direct me to inquire about conducting a Bible study for Teen Challenge. *Father,* I thought, *I'm already doing a weekly program at the Salvation Army.* But I called the Administrator, Raul, and asked if they allowed outsiders to lead a Bible study. I mentioned that I was already leading a study at the Salvation Army. He said, "Sure, come on over!" We set a time and I added that to my schedule.

My ministry schedule became pretty hectic. Tuesday was the Army. Wednesday was Teen Challenge from 2-4 pm, and I was also leading a Bible study at our A-1 office from 4:30-6 pm. I was also a life group leader for First Assembly of God, which met at our home from 7-9 pm.

Prayer Rocks

One day something happened that altered the way I looked at prayer. In 1994, I had attended my first Hawaiian Islands Ministries conference at the 'Ilikai Hotel. I heard a missionary speaker, Marilyn Laszlo, tell of her journey into Papua New Guinea. They had taken a boat trip down the river to gather supplies. The trip home was four days long and they knew they needed five cans of gas to make it back home.

However, they discovered that they had only four cans as someone had forgotten to fill the fifth can. She knew what lay ahead: they would run out of gas a half-a-day's journey from home and would be forced to drift back to town for fresh supplies. And that meant they faced drifting on the river an additional eight or nine days. It was a dangerous predicament but one they couldn't do anything about.

Suddenly, one of the natives was struck by a brilliant idea: They could pray and God would get them home. The missionary confessed that she didn't have enough faith for this prayer so she told the native, "Good, you pray." So he did. He laid his hands on the engine and prayed that God would get them home. Miraculously, they made it home without that fifth tank of gas.

My engineering mind calculated that there were only two logical answers to the missionary's miracle: Either she lied or she had told the truth. The Bible tells us that God does all kinds of miracles and supernatural feats, even in our physical world. I decided to believe that God could do the miraculous and God tested my faith.

A Test of My Faith

One day, I was leaving Teen Challenge and got to the 20-foot gate that blocked the road. The lock was the largest one I had ever seen.

When I tried to open the lock, my key didn't fit. I turned it upside-down to see if anything was stuck inside, but it looked fine. I tried again and again, with no success.

Then I remembered that missionary and thought, *If it worked for them, it could work for me!* It sounds dopey but it was already 4:10 pm and I had no other choice. If I went back, I would be late for the A-1 Bible study. So I laid my hands on the lock and prayed: "Father, please open this lock." I tried again, to no success. I prayed the same prayer over again and tried the lock, but again, no success.

At this point, I panicked. I was locked in and it was almost 4:15 pm. So I laid my hands on the lock for the third time and prayed again, then slowly pushed the key in. It opened!

God did something to unlock my unbelief and increase my faith. After that I started praying for simple things in the physical realm.

Praying for Little Things

The first thing I began praying for was parking. One Christmas at Ala Moana parking was especially tight. It was the week before Christmas, early on a Saturday afternoon, prime shopping time! Cars were circling the lot like wolves. As we cruised the south side, we passed Makai Market (the food court), and I prayed that a stall would open up for us. This would be a minor miracle as there were only about 15 stalls, the sweetest spot of the lot. However, a parking stall opened up as soon as we turned the corner! Diana and I believed God answered our prayer.

After that incident, I pray for parking wherever I go. Parking might seem to be a small thing. I don't believe God is sitting in heaven just waiting to provide parking, but I do believe He can answer whatever He desires, big or small. After all, He created the atom,

He can answer whatever He desires, big or small

the DNA helix, our feelings, smell and taste, and light. Is anything too hard for God Almighty? Should we wait for only impossible situations to pray for God to intervene or should we ask Him to provide the simple things?

God's Word tells us: *"Delight yourself in the Lord and he will give you the desires of your heart"* (PSALM 37:4). Does this apply to parking too? The biggest impact that praying has made on my life is to create a disciplined life of dependence on God.

Calling On Jesus

Another situation advanced this belief to call on God in all things. One of our project managers, Sam Nonaka, got into an accident on the freeway. A car had spun around on the freeway and ended up heading straight towards his car. It hit his car, scraping the entire right side. The day after the accident, I asked Sam if he had cried out to Jesus. Sam answered, "No!"

I wondered if I would have called on Jesus instinctively. I resolved to practice and call out to Jesus the next time I got injured.

About a month later, I smashed one of my fingers in my car door. I immediately grabbed my finger and said, "Jesus! Please ease the pain!" This was a prayer request, not an angry swearing or "use-God's-name-in-vain." I was so delighted with my newfound faith that I remember rejoicing and forgot all about my banged-up finger. After a few more "mini-mishaps" – slamming fingers in doors, spraining toes, banging my head on objects – my prayer life and dependence on God grew stronger. I felt the pleasure of God each time I reacted in a prayerful way.

I felt the pleasure of God each time I reacted in a prayerful way.

34

Can God Strum a Guitar?

During my six-year involvement with Teen Challenge, there was a special event that occurred after the second year. I have a passion for teaching apologetics – presenting evidence for the existence of God. My teachings came in large part from the book, *Evidence that Demands a Verdict*. On this day, I had arrived early and the group was out at a worship outreach so no one was at the camp.

Just after 2 pm, the van drove up and the group gathered in our usual circle. There were about 10 students. One of the guys had a guitar he had brought back from the worship session, and he rested it against a tree about five feet away.

Our focus for the day was how we can be sure God exists. We drew evidence from three major areas:

I.   We can see God's *"awesome power and divine nature from what he has created"* (ROMANS 1:20).

II.   We can understand that God exists because of the historic fact that Jesus died and rose again. Additionally, there is historic record of the existence and actions of the disciples also known as the apostles. Would they die for a lie? Would they write the stories (gospels) of Jesus' many miracles and His death for our wrongs, and then go to their own deaths knowing what they wrote was a lie? Impossible!

III. We can also see God's divine nature in the Bible. There are many proven prophecies about Jesus and Israel all throughout God's written Word.

After spending several weeks leading up to this session, it was now "graduation." The Bible says that if a person truly believes in Jesus Christ:

- *Who He is – God in the flesh,*

- *What He did – He died for us,*

- *Why He died – to pay a price we could not pay for our own sins,*

- *How we have assurance that God the Father accepted Jesus' price – He raised Jesus from the dead,*

Then if we confess with our mouth Jesus as Lord, we become sons of God and enter into an eternal relationship with the Father through Jesus Christ.

All evangelicals (or believers) have different prayers that include essential elements. God teaches these elements in His Word so that a person seeking a relationship with Him can pray and enter into His Kingdom. On this particular day, I chose a 10-word prayer that was easy to remember while containing the essentials of confessing Jesus as Lord. Here is that prayer to Jesus:

> I'm a sinner,
> Please forgive me,
> Come; be my Lord,
> Thanks.

Then I added, "If you can't remember that, here's a four-word prayer: *'I trust in Jesus!'*"

The instant I said "Jesus," the guitar that was against the tree and about five feet away from the closest person, went off. Someone or something gave a solid, open-frat strum on the guitar. The person on my right, Dan W., pointed to the guitar and said, "Did you hear that?" I looked and saw the guitar in its original position. No one had touched it, there was no wind, and it had not fallen down. And, even more eerily, the guitar didn't move. It was as still as if nothing had happened, and yet we had all clearly heard it.

We all understood that God moved that day and somehow strummed the guitar. Whether it was an angel, or whether He just spoke, His supernatural hand was evident. As amazing as that was, the real joy came in realizing that I was exactly where God wanted me to be, doing what He wanted me to do. I felt His pleasure in my soul.

I felt His pleasure in my soul.

Proud father(Jimmy Sr) and son(Jimmy boy)-1949

Jimmy boy-one year old

Ronnie(brother) and Jimmy-1952

Enokawa Family-1951

Hiro(brother) and Diana-1949

Impalas-1960
Front-Larry Ueki,George Matsuda, Melvin Goto, Carl Yorita,
Greg DelaSantos
2nd-Alvin Young, Jimmy, Mike Kawamoto, Melvin Takahashi,
Roy Tsumoto, Keith Tsubota
3rd-Ben Fujimoto, our Advisor, Carl Yanagihara

Diana Enokawa-Miss Cutest

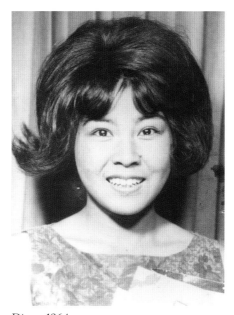

Diana-1964

Yamadas-1977

Jimmy-Stoned(I had hair)

Jimmy-Trying to look cool

Jimmy, Diana, Ma and Pop Enokawa-1973

Diana-Happily Married(Honeymoon)

Mom Yamada, Jimmy, Ma Enokawa-1987

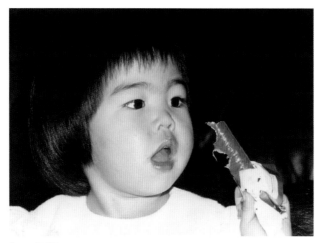

Lisa-1987

Daven (left) and the Epic Sessions

Yamada Kids and Mom

Safaris-2007
Front-Daven Morikawa, Lloyd Fujie
Back-Melvin Takahashi, Ben Fujimoto, Wally Hirai

Safaris-2007
Front-Keith Ogata, Paul Tomonari, Jimmy
Back-Alvin Young, Lorrin Kunimoto, Larry Ueki, Mike Kawamoto

Yamadas and the Bauers-2006
Front-Diana and Jimmy, Tom and Cindy Bauer
Back-Christy, Daven, Lisa, Charis, Chari

Front-Donna, Jessica, Lisa, Charity
Back-Jason, Jimmy, Diana, Daven

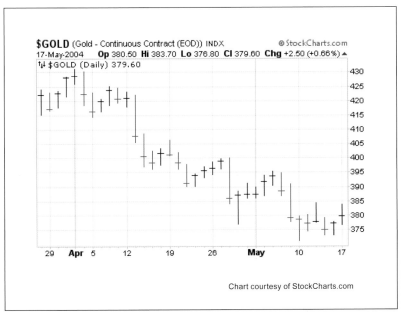

On April 5, 2004, God gave me a dream that gold would fall by $60.

On April 27, 2003, God gave me a dream to buy the S&P500 Index. The buy signal was guidance from God to close out our S&P hedge.

5

Walking On Water

Supernatural High: Surfing

My first wave was a memorable one that avalanched into a major ministry, which is why I'll never forget it: It was all of one foot high.

It was the summer of 1963 and Alvin Y. took us surfing. We were just outside the beach at the Wailupe Fire Station. My board was a loaner, one of those old tankers: a 10-footer, water-logged and full of dings.

I had taken off on a small wave that eventually broke and turned into whitewater. Better surfers jump off the wave at that point but there was no way I was jumping off this baby. I had paddled too hard to get to the takeoff point in the lineup and waited too long for it. No one gives a "gremmie" beginner a chance, so I had to make it for myself.

This was the best wave of my life; I was screaming as I rode the wave all the way in. I was stoked, experienced the feeling that only surfers can feel. Then and there I was hooked on surfing. I can still picture the ride: standing up, trying to keep my balance, my board flying across the wave and riding high on white water.

A Season to Surf

Surfing made high school and college seem like the best times of my life. Life couldn't get any better: I had the Safaris to hang with, Diana to hold hands with, good grades to keep my parents happy, and my '57 Chevy for cruising. I surfed as often as I could, mostly at Ala Moana Beach Park.

Those were the days when the boards didn't have leashes and if you lost your board, you swam. On big surf days, with waves over three feet high, you learned to "turtle" which meant turning your board over and clinging to it with your hands and feet. Then you hung on for life. There is nothing worse than having a set of waves come in as you paddle out, and having your board ripped out of your hands. Then you not only missed the set and you're embarrassed because you got killed by a wave, and when you finally paddle back out, your friends ask you where you've been.

Even though we grew up in Hawai'i, everything was still seasonal. We played sports from fourth grade through high school, then surfed and shot pool from high school through college. The Safaris played poker and some of us even took up bridge. But as with all things, those seasons came to an end (except we still play poker—adding Texas Hold 'em for fun). I stopped surfing when I found booze, drugs, and women.

Walking on Water…Again

It was Jason who resurrected surfing for me. (Actually it was body boarding, but I'll call it surfing.) Jason's interest shifted from fishing to body boarding when he turned 13. Every weekend after judo the family headed to the beach. Jason and I would be in the surf at Waimanalo Beach, while the rest of the family played on the shore. When Jason improved, we graduated to the more challenging waves at Kewalo Basin, next to Ala Moana Beach. Daven joined us and thoroughly enjoyed it.

Later, when Jason started driving and no longer wanted dad for his surfing escapades, Daven joined me and we went surfing several times each week. Surfing became our exercise. After I became a Christian in 1993, I fondly remember one Easter break when Daven and I surfed for eight days straight. Eventually, however, even Daven got his first car and didn't need his dad anymore.

Board Meeting

In the summer of 1997, I was surfing at Kewalo's at a break called "The Point." The better, more aggressive surfers surfed there and they let me join in as I was a generous surfer. I always gave the crowd the first and even second waves. My strategy was I would then have the third wave to myself. Not only was this good from the Christian standpoint of sharing, it was also good strategy for getting the best waves.

I was in the lineup talking to my friend Leon when another guy paddled over. "There's Tom," Leon said. As Tom paddled up, I said, "Tom, long time no see!" Tom looked puzzled. I continued, "Oh, man, have you forgotten me already?" Tom opened his hands wide, puzzled and apologized, whereupon Leon and I broke out in laughter. Tom was actually a great practical joker and he realized he had just been "punked"!

Tom was a missionary with an organization called Youth With a Mission (YWAM). He was only visiting for couple of weeks, helping a church fix up a property in Kalihi Valley, and then on his way to Australia. We connected since he was a pastor and a brother in the Lord. I pondered how one could live the way he was living, just trusting God all the way. No solid job, no medical insurance, no retirement, just faith.

After my surf session, I was about to leave the parking lot when I noticed Tom sitting in the front seat of Leon's car. I felt God tell me to go and give Tom some money, so I jumped out and knocked on his window. Tom looked up, surprised. "God wanted me to bless you," I explained as I handed over the cash.

As I drove home, I stopped by a Jack-in-the-Box to get Diana her favorite coffee. As I was waiting in the drive-through, Leon drove into a parking stall opposite my car. I thought, *Look at this guy! Tom gets a few dollars and he's buying breakfast!*

God: "Help Them!"

As I drove home, I had a picture in my mind, which I now can call a vision from God. I saw one of those old green plantation homes with a metal roof and an old electrical service. (Forgive me, I'm an electrician at heart!) I felt the Lord tell me to help Tom fix up the church property he was working on. I told the Lord that and if He wanted me to help, He would have to make a connection with Tom.

A month later, there was a statewide men's event at our church. I was certain God would make the connection with Tom. At the event, I watched for Tom, knowing his silver-white hair would surely stand out. I was disappointed when I didn't connect with him that day but I was certain that it would happen in God's perfect time.

Lisa's Wild Goose Chase

In the summer of 1998, our daughter Lisa wanted to attend a Christian concert in Kalihi Valley. I told her I was not familiar with any place in Kalihi where they could hold a large concert, but volunteered to take them. We drove up to a location about a mile above Kamehameha Shopping Center. The winding road was very dark and unsafe. I was certain it was a wild goose chase, but what did I know? The facility's lights glared over the parking lot and loud music blared into the silent night. We hesitantly dropped the group off and told them we would return at 10 pm.

We returned a little early so we could check out the festivities. The room where the concert was being held seemed small for what looked like 150 or so kids. We took the girls to eat saimin at Kelly's Restaurant. Lisa told us that the place was so hot that someone fainted during the concert, dropping like a sack of potatoes right on the floor.

God Orchestrates Little Things

The year 1998 was a good year for Daven and his spiritual growth. I was a life group leader and our study drew Daven's friends. I encouraged him to start a small Bible study of his own since his friend's parents might stop his friends from attending a "play night" in the middle of the week, especially when they got home at 10 pm. Daven took my advice and when we stopped our life group in September, his Bible study took off.

By early 1999, Daven's group grew to a regular attendance of 10-15 high school students. They arrived around 6:30 pm and could swim and play basketball, ping-pong, or TV games. At 7 pm, we served dinner which alternated between steak and chicken, salmon and chicken, and always, the must-have pizza. The kids loved these basics, no matter how often we served them. After dinner, they had worship which was lead by Daven, and then a short Bible study which ended around 8:30 pm. After that the fun festivities started up again until we closed down around 9:30 pm.

In March, Daven told us he was going to the senior prom. Prior to this he had never dated nor gone to any proms in four years at high school. He had been too busy surfing.

Diana and I were happy for him and asked who he was going with. He told us about a girl named Christy, who had just attended his Bible study for the second time the night before. The next week, I made it a point to find out who she was. An opportunity arose after the Bible study. She told me her dad was a pastor named Tom at Grace Bible, formerly a YWAM missionary. He had been en route to Australia when he was asked to help repair their property. A light bulb went on. I asked if her dad surfed at Kewalo's. She answered, "Sometimes."

I knew God had made the connection I had asked for over a year and a half earlier.

"Does he surf with a long board?" I pressed.

"Well, yes," she replied.

I knew God had made the connection I had asked for over a year and a half earlier.

"Tell your dad that I'm the surfer who gave him some money in the summer of 1997," I instructed her, and asked for his phone number. I called the next day and found out he was indeed the very same Tom. It seemed unbelievable but I realize nothing is too difficult for God. Tom Bauer and his wife Cindy had four daughters – Carla, Christy, Cari and Charis.

When I went to meet the Bauers in 1999, I realized that the concert had been the Bauer's church event, the year before.

These two seemingly unrelated stories tied us to the Bauers and showed me that God wanted this connection to be solid.

God Changes, But Doesn't End Relationships

What God builds, He can change, rebuild, break down or stop. Most of what He does is seasonal with a beginning and an end, just like life. Daven's small Bible study soon grew into a large group. It was an open invitation and eventually became a Grace Bible outreach averaging 30 to 40 kids, and occasionally drawing 50. Once it even hit 80! That night we served four large pieces of salmon, four 8-by-12 inch pans of lasagna, twelve pounds of barbecue chicken, twelve large pizzas, and of course, drinks. And for dessert Diana served her famous pound cake. Nothing was left over. Diana wondered whether the lanai would hold what was surely 10,000 pounds of people!

God was doing many things through the various Bible studies: kids were giving their lives to Jesus, leaders were being developed, and many of the youth were reaching out to others. There was power in the growing numbers. However, what touched me most was the worship. Although it was short, these teenagers worshipped God with all of their heart, soul, mind, and strength.

There was power in the growing numbers.

By March of 2003, the Bible study was five years old. I don't know what it was that made me realize a change was coming, but I told Tom. I wasn't sure what it looked like and when, but I knew God was stirring, I could feel it in my soul.

God's Dream Team

By late June, there was a move in our church for men to connect. One Saturday, on July 19, 2003, there were three events to choose from. Youth For Christ Hawai'i (YFCH) had a final volleyball tournament competition. Then there was a Harvest Crusade with Pastor Greg Laurie at the Waikiki Shell. And finally, our church was hosting a men's fellowship barbecue. I chose the barbeque. Pastor Ko shared about the men making a stronger connection in the church and taking greater leadership roles in the family.

At Sunday service, Pastor Ko preached a similar message. I was moved but still resisted because I was already involved: I had a men's monthly gathering and felt a little smug about it. I was already active. Trusting God, I prayed, "Lord, if you really want me to be more involved, give me a dream tonight about the men in our church."

That night I had a dream involving Pastor Ko and Pastor Ernie. (Pastor Ernie had prayed the salvation prayer with me on June 6, 1993.) In the dream, we were at our A-1 warehouse and Pastor Ko climbed up one of the posts holding up the warehouse, then held on tightly at the top. The dream shifted to Pastor Ernie and me. We were holding one end of a ten-foot length of four-inch rigid conduit (metal pipe used for electrical wiring), weighing approximately 50 pounds. We were running as if we were racing another team, though there was no one else. After ten feet, we suddenly dropped the conduit, the dream ended and I awoke.

I realized God had given me direction and the interpretation was clear. We were letting men in the church fall through our grasps. I called the church the next day and before I could say anything about my dream, Tom's wife Cindy informed me that God impressed upon her that He wanted to move the Bible study to Kalihi, in the larger room where they held concerts. I then explained the events of the past weekend which culminated in the dream on Sunday night. Her idea to move the study only confirmed what God was directing us to prepare us for a season of growth. At that time, Tom was in Bali on a month-long mission trip. When Tom returned in August we started the new study. It was bittersweet, a time of rejoicing and a time of crying.

6

God's War Package

Youth For Christ: God Speaks if We Listen

Youth for Christ (YFC) is an evangelical organization that was formed in the 1950s. It reaches out to high school students through many venues and its impact is nationwide. In fact, one of its very first evangelists was "The Evangelist," Billy Graham.

Our son Daven was in seventh grade at Moanalua Intermediate when a friend invited him to a volleyball tournament. I took Daven that very first day and met a staff person by the name of Keli'i. Before this, I had written a brief ten-page booklet entitled, "Christian War Package." It was a means of sharing the Gospel without forcing people to listen for hours to all of the evidence for God's existence. I was passionate about sharing the Gospel and gave this "CWP" to everyone I met.

When I met Keli'i, I gave him the "War Package." I shared with him my strong belief that the youth needed to have solid evidence for God's existence. Had I known that Keli'i was in fact Keli'i Akina, the executive director of Youth for Christ in Hawai'i who had served in YFC for approximately 15 years, I would have buttoned my mouth.

However, the positive result of that insensitive act was that a few years later, YFC was expanding their Board of Directors and my name came up. Keli'i tied my name to that overly bold Christian who had given him a crudely written "War Package." Keli'i and Terry Bosgra invited me to lunch and asked me to join YFC's Board. I initially declined but prayed on the matter, and eventually accepted. The year was 1999 and this was to become a divine connection for the future of the War Package.

Columbine Hits Home

April has always been a very good month for me since both Diana and Jason were born in April. However what took place on April 20, 1999 marred April that year. On that day, two students massacred 13 victims at Columbine High School. My heart was distressed and God used that to spur me into action.

My heart was distressed and God used that to spur me into action.

I was doing my morning devotion, a time when I stretch my body and listen to God via either a message on a Christian station KLHT (1040 AM) or listen to worship music. Both help me start the day with a focus on God. By the time I get to work, I've usually spent between an hour to an hour and a half with Him. On that day, in my devotions, I had a vision (a daydream) of myself on the Moanalua High School campus at what is known as "Menehune Square," sharing the Gospel with the youth.

A month later, at a Saturday morning men's breakfast, I was with a Vietnamese Christian, Moses Cao. When Moses laid his hands on me and prayed, I received the same vision. As I reflected on these two events, I knew God was telling me that instead of just being angry, I needed to do something about Columbine.

Penetrating the High Schools

Soon after, I wrote a letter to a friend, the principal of Moanalua High School expressing how terrible the Columbine tragedy was and how I hoped to make a difference. All I needed was a corner on campus to share the Gospel with the students. I believed that if they heard the message, it would make the school a better place. I admit that, it was overly naïve, but I believed it came from God and I was simply obeying what He was telling me.

> I admit that, it was overly naïve, but I believed it came from God and I was simply obeying what He was telling me.

The principal responded that due to the separation of church and state, she could not allow me to come on campus for that purpose. This was the first time I had heard this, but it wouldn't be the last. She did say, however, that if I wanted to pursue the matter I could contact the Assistant District Superintendent.

So I did. First I called him then I sent him the same letter I had sent to the principal. He told me the same thing. And again, his negative response held a small silver lining of hope: I could pursue the matter by going to the next level and contacting the Assistant Attorney General.

So I did!

The Assistant Attorney General replied with the best answer yet: He said I might be able to use the flagpole, an area designated for the freedom of speech. What a great idea! I was excited and encouraged by the thought that this could open the door for many groups to have access to the public school system, simply by witnessing at the flagpole. So I sent my letter off. After months of phone calls and no results, I thought, *Well, at least I tried!*

Mission to March!

Months later, I went to see the movie, "Mission to Mars." In it, Earth sends a space team to investigate strange supernatural events on Mars. They discover a gorgeous female Martian who shows them a DNA helix, which she then puts on their spaceship to return to Earth. It crashes in the ocean, then an amoeba turns into a fish, which turns into a reptile, then into a bison and eventually into a man. The spaceman says, "Of course, that's how it all began." I had really been enjoying the movie up to that point, but suddenly my heart burned with anger.

I remembered being blinded by a similar scene in the Disney movie, "Fantasia." I knew that millions of people who had seen the film would be brainwashed the same way, believe in macroevolution and not even know why. God spoke to my heart: "What are you going to do about it?" I jumped up and started drawing a series of pictures that laid out the concept for an apologetics "comic book." This booklet would present evidence for the existence of God in three areas.

The Bible says, *"The god of this age [Satan] has blinded the minds of unbelievers, so that they cannot see the light of the gospel of the glory of Christ..."* (2 CORINTHIANS 4:4). The booklet was to counter Satan's attack. Why? Because whatever God states to be true, if that truth is important in understanding God, Satan goes against it. And so here are the three areas I targeted:

I.   The Bible tells us that God created the universe. Satan blinds us with the idea that the universe evolved, and with it life forms evolved, so that something was created from nothing.

II. God says that Jesus died and rose again. Satan comes through the media, educational system, and the wisdom of the world and says Jesus was a good man but He did not rise from the dead. Authors write books in their areas of expertise, often laughing at the idea of Jesus' resurrection and why they don't believe it. Then the media prints their beliefs, often as truth.

III.   God says the Bible was written by God through men who wrote as *"they were carried along by the Holy Spirit"* (2 PETER 1:20-21). Satan tells us that the Bible is full of errors, that men wrote it, and that it is continually changing.

After half an hour or so, I had finished some crude sketches and the general idea. *Now what?* I wondered. I remembered a meeting I had a year earlier with Alfredo Garma, a graphic artist. Since this new booklet would involve pictures, graphics would be the highlight. At the time, Alfredo was working with high school students on the "X Magazine," which he also distributed to high schools. I met with Alfredo and his wife and they were interested. After a year, we developed a booklet that exceeded my expectations. As I thought about going to print, I considered approaching Keli'i Akina to ask whether YFCH would be interested in assisting in distribution.

Keli'i was interested, but felt the booklet needed to be modified to reduce its strong anti-evolutionary stance. I learned that God can improve what you are doing if you let Him. So I gave Keli'i our preliminary copy and waited. Keli'i and a team made the changes.

> *I learned that God can improve what you are doing if you let Him.*

God Goes BIG: Partnering with Campus Crusade

Keli'i received a call one day from Campus Crusade, an evangelical organization founded by Bill Bright that also reached out to high schools. They had received a $750,000 grant to help with the distribution of "The Jesus Video" to every residence in Hawai'i. They asked if Keli'i and YFCH wanted to participate in what was to be the largest and most aggressive evangelism project in our state's history.

Keli'i 'happened' to be 20 minutes away from the Campus Crusade headquarters in Los Angeles; he said, "I'll be right over!"

God's hand was apparent. They discussed the project and talked about materials to be a included in the project. Keli'i "happened" to have the booklet with him and showed it to the group. Eventually approximately 80,000 copies of the booklet were distributed as part of the Jesus Project, along with almost 400,000 copies of "The Jesus Video." That started with a voice from God to speak to students in Menehune Square.

God's big projects often start with a small act of obedience. It's about taking one small first step. Abraham, Moses, Joseph, Nehemiah, Judah, and Esther all started

God's big projects often start with a small act of obedience.

their big projects with a first little step. And God used that act of obedience to come alongside them and show Himself to them and through them.

God Turns Prejudice to Friendship

One of the things that makes Hawai'i so special is its aloha spirit. While integration and busing in the school systems was a big problem for most of the United States, its impact in Hawai'i was minimal. But that didn't mean prejudice wasn't here too. If you were a Caucasian ("*haole*") in areas like Waianae or Waimanalo, things were rough for you. Even if you were Hawaiian, you experienced hidden prejudice. I didn't think I had any prejudice toward Hawaiians as they were the true locals and I had known a number of them while I was growing up.

One day Pastor Daniel Kikawa spoke at our church. His focus was how the God of Creation was the first God of Hawai'i. Something made me realize I had a prejudice against Hawaiians. I knew a number of Hawaiians and loved them dearly. A prejudice, however, goes beyond liking a few people. Prejudice is disliking a racial group without knowing anything about them. It's a negative opinion based on race.

Daniel was with a group called *Aloha Ke Akua* (Love the Lord) and was set to speak further on the same topic later that evening. Realizing my prejudice touched a nerve in me, so I went to meet him. I got to know him well and quickly became interested in helping him distribute his book, *Perpetuated in Righteousness*. Over the next few months, I also got caught up in another one of his projects: a video on God in Japan. God used these connections to bring me alongside Daniel so that I would partner with him and also to develop another project, the Japanese War Package.

Japanese War Package

The idea that God revealed himself to the Japanese in their culture intrigued me. So I laid a fleece out for the Lord: if I could assemble a strong team to accomplish the effort, God was indeed telling me to launch a second War Package. This time for a country!

After a few months, we had assembled the team: Alfredo Garma—graphics, Daniel Kikawa—a few sections, Kevin Asano—one section, Junji Ono—Japanese national and a pastor who would help with overall editing, Brooks Infante—a high school student and artist with an eye for drawing Japanese characters, and myself.

We met for about a year and a half. After many hours of input and discussion over what to include, how to approach the subject, and necessary changes, the most powerful lesson was not about Japan, but about ourselves. As Christians from different churches and denominations, we learned to work together by putting our differences aside.

There was always unity in our spirit. With unity, God was able to take the product and, with his Holy Spirit, bring His power into it. About 2,000 copies of the booklet were distributed and to this day I count the project a spiritual success.

Yet Another War Package

One night as I was checking e-mail, I received one from Pastor Ted Kawabata. He was thinking of supporting a missionary from Victory Campus Ministry. I don't know what interested me but I called the number on the e-mail immediately. It was 9 pm Hawai'i Standard Time. The phone rang a couple of times and Daniel answered. We talked for a few minutes and then we were disconnected.

Two days later, Daniel called to apologize. I had called his cell phone while they were sleeping at home. I apologized for calling so late, explaining that I hadn't realized what time zone I was calling. He explained how it had been an anointed call: his wife was pregnant and when I called, she went into labor. They had a baby boy that morning!

I've learned when something unusual happens, God is probably involved: listen as he may be either speaking or guiding. *"In his heart a man plans his course, but the Lord determines his steps"* (PROVERBS 16:9). Over the next few weeks, I kept asking the Lord to reveal what it was He wanted me to do.

"In his heart a man plans his course, but the Lord determines his steps" (PROVERBS 16:9).

I felt Him tell me to read up on China so I read *Jesus in Beijing* by David Aikmen, *The Heavenly Man* by Brother Yun and Paul Hattaway, and *Back to Jerusalem* by Paul Hattaway. I then felt the Lord release me to produce a Chinese War Package. Again I assembled a team, which included Daniel Kikawa, an expert in indigenous cultures; Alfredo Garma, graphic designer; Ginger Chock; Greg and Fawn Anderman; and myself.

Ginger Chock was an expert in the history of Chinese language going all the way back to the early turtle shell carvings. She had even written two books on the subject. Greg Anderman was a television producer who had developed a few specials on the topic, including one revealing that the God of the Bible was in many Chinese rituals. Fawn, his wife, was a Chinese national involved in Chinese journalism.

With our team assembled, we proceeded to meet and develop the concept for the booklet. We met six times over eight months. But at the end of that period, I felt the Lord tell me to stop. In my research of what was already available to the Chinese, I found an enormous amount of Christian resources. We could have continued and created something original but I'm not sure God would have been the guiding hand behind it. I remember being in prayer, sitting outside a heath store, when God clearly told me to stop the project. The eight months had not been a waste; in fact, He had heightened my awareness of China's importance in the last days.

Underground Revolution

Up until summer 2005, China had had two major Christian groups: an underground church and the state-controlled church, "The Three Self Church." There were possibly 15 million in the Three Self Church and as many as 100 million in the underground church.

The underground church had been born out of efforts of the missionaries in China from 1850-1900, like Hudson Taylor, CT Studd, and the Cambridge Seven.

However, the Christians in China underwent tremendous persecution during Mao's Cultural Revolution. Possibly over a million Christians died – exact statistics are hard to come by. After the persecution, they reorganized how they selected their leaders in the '80s and '90s. Finally, the underground church experienced enough freedom to gather and grow. Many times they asked one another how long they had been in jail during the persecution. The longest was for over 20 years. However, these same persecuted prisoners emerged as the new spiritual leaders of the burgeoning underground church.

This rich history in such an ancient and venerated culture will surely come in to play in the coming times. Further, God's War Package had already been drafted in English and then distributed statewide. Then it was translated into Japanese and promised to go into many other countries.

While I was blown away by the potential of the Gospel going to every corner of the world, I also had to wonder: *What else could God have up His sleeve?*

7

Going to All Nations

God Opens Thailand

In the summer of 2005, I met a couple who would become the next chapter of my ministry: Terry and Peggy Schmitt. At the time, Pastor Daniel Kikawa had put together an indigenous peoples' worship conference that drew people from all over the world. Indigenous Christians are very close to their original culture and worship Jesus in a way relevant to that culture.

The Schmitts had come from Thailand. Pastor Daniel had asked a few of us to host some of the indigenous conference attendees. God selected Diana and me to host Terry and Peggy. A few days before the conference, Tom Bauer and I had lunch with Terry and Peggy. They were involved in a multi-faceted ministry; one of its main missions ministered to Thai children involved in human trafficking. They were sold into prostitution. The money is tremendous for those on the profit end of the deal. For the children, it was extremely traumatic.

During lunch we discovered that it was a wedding anniversary for Terry and Peggy. God put in my heart to give them a little vacation at the 'Ihilani Resort with the use of a car. They enjoyed their time in Hawai'i, and when they left we stayed connected via e-mail.

Miracle Money

Most of our e-mail correspondence kept me abreast of the Schmitts' ministry. On Saturday, March 11, 2005, I received an e-mail about an opportunity for Peggy. Justice for Children International (JFCI) had an intensive nine-month seminar where a student earned the equivalent of a Masters degree in caring for children caught in forced child prostitution. The graduates were fully licensed and equipped to help the youth when they broke free. The e-mail specifically requested a few things:

> "Please pray for the needed $7,000 for [Peggy] to attend. She will also need approximately $1,500 for airfare plus expenses while in Connecticut."

> Pray Peggy is given favor by the selection committee of Justice For Children Int'l (sic). [Also, please pray that] Peggy would be able to set up a child counseling center at the Int'l church we attend here in Chiang Mai...."

I replied in the following e-mail:

> "Terry... Can you handle 9 months without Peggy? I don't know if I could survive 1 month without Diana! What people of faith!

> You have the money...

> You don't have the time...

> Did you submit your application yet? The deadline

was March 1. Where is Peggy staying in CT while she attends the program?

Terry sent back this response:

"Can you handle 9 months without Peggy?
NOT EASILY

I don't know if I could survive 1 month without Diana…
FORTUNATELY I'LL BE IN THE U.S. TILL THE
END OF SEPT.…

What people of faith…YES

You have the money…HAVE, BUT IN THIS CASE,
MORE IS BETTER

You don't have the time…HAVE

Did you submit your application yet? The deadline
was March 1. ALREADY; WAITING TO HEAR
FROM JFCI.

Where is Peggy staying in CT while she attends the
program? WITH A FAMILY IN NEW HAVEN.

He added:

Jimmy… Peggy has wanted to further her education for
years but this is the first time she knows it is right as the
Lord is directing her into child counseling [and] nobody
is doing this here in a consistent way. Of course, there is
mega abuse of children…we are almost tired of the sad
stories. Peggy is a children's nurse by training & trains up

[others] as well [for] restricted nations in Asia so it is a good fit. We so appreciate your interest enough to ask the questions. We know he will make this come about as it is for his Kingdom work and glory. It seems we are constantly running into people who are wounded, even those on the field. This week alone Peggy ministered mind renewal to one missionary and to one short-term missionary.

Keep us in your prayers, Jimmy & Diana, and we will do the same for you…

Yours in Him,
Terry

I replied by asking how much they had in their overall budget. He sent me back the following e-mail on the very next day, Sunday, March 12, 2005:

Child Counseling Course	COSTS:	
Nine-month Course Fee	$	7,000
Airfare	$	1,500
MN to CT travel	$	350
Lodging in CT		
Groceries: 6 mos. ($70/mo.)	$	420
Personal care: 9 mos. ($35/mo.)	$	315
City bus/incidentals	$	150
Bicycle/helmet	$	275
Total	$	10,010

Know at this time:

1. Peggy has applied for a scholarship from JFCI; no word yet on this or acceptance into the program course.

2. We do have the $1,500 & $1,100 for the air ticket – we've taken from our own account as we saved up for these costs.

3. IF Peggy receives a JFCI scholarship & IF her church will continue to pay her monthly salary, she will simply need help to take care of additional travel costs & incidental/ bicycle and the like.

4. Should Peggy for some reason NOT be accepted into the JFCI course her year is basically blown as far as scheduling ministry as she has turned down offers in hopes of attending the JFCI program.

After receiving this detailed e-mail and seeing their preparation, Diana and I made a contribution. I sent a response to Peggy after she informed us that she was accepted:

Terry & Peggy...

Great news: God is in control!

When do you need the funds? To whom do we cut the check?

Just wanted to share how God spoke to me. I find so often that God's gentle voice is a journey... Last year, Diana and I went to New York for a vacation. While we were there, we saw a TV movie about kidnapping/selling of kids into prostitution. Since we rarely watch TV, we would never have seen the movie had we not been in NY.

The day I got Terry's e-mail...I felt a gentle nudge. However, as with everyone, my plate is full. Among other support of ministries, we are trying to help the Bauers (Surfing the Nations) buy the property they are living on. I'm trying to cut back on various supports so I'm ready for the purchase of the property.

Since I felt the nudge, I pulled up the site for JFCI & found that Lamont Hiebert is Executive Director. I have his CDs: "Dreams of God," and others he did with a group called Ten Shekels Shirt. After I printed info from the site, I sat at my table and was studying, listening to the radio (unusual, I usually have a CD playing), and a song from "Dreams of God" came on. Because there are different artists on the CD, I ran to my room to look at who wrote and performed the song playing. It was none other than Lamont Hiebert (Song: "We Make A Way"). When I saw the connection, I thought, *Okay, God, if you want me to help Peggy, give me a dream tonight (still Saturday).*

That night I dreamt about my daughter Lisa, currently at Pepperdine University. Diana had been concerned about her since she's living on her own…if someone kidnaps her, no one would know. In the dream, we're at a party, and one of her male friends came and told me how Lisa is the "life of the party" (not a good picture) and then says one word to me: "Spooky." When I awoke, I realized he said that because there were strangers at the party. It was clear then that God wanted me to partner with you.

Bottom line: WE HAVE AN AWESOME GOD!

Agape…
Jimmy

I realized in the dream that if Lisa got into trouble, it might have been her decision. But children who are kidnapped and sold as sex slaves were not responsible for what happened to them.

God can speak in dreams and visions, if you desire that he communicate with you in this manner. Here's a question: Did people in the Old Testament have dreams as often as we do? Is it possible that they didn't?

Both the Old Testament prophet Joel and Peter in the New Testament tell us, "*Young men will see visions, old men will dream dreams*" (ACTS 2:17). Not all dreams contain lessons from God; however, is it possible that all dreams are sent from God? Science may know what part of the brain generates dreams, but do we know if the brain can make up its own dreams? Could they be "sent" from God? I believe they are.

The Bible tells us that wisdom is from God (DANIEL 2:23 – God gave Daniel wisdom). It also says that God gives wisdom to the man who pleases him (ECCLESIASTES 2:26). For example, God gave wisdom to King Solomon (2 CHRONICLES 1:11-12). And there is a clear case of God speaking in a dream in the book of Job (JOB 33:14-15).

If wisdom is making the right choice in any situation, then how does God give that ability to a person? First, he gives humans a brain. He also gives the knowledge of his Word. And how about this scenario: Could God "download" information into our minds via a wireless communication system He set up at the beginning of time? If so, could that be what we know as dreams?

Logic and theology aside, I believe that not all wisdom or dreams are from God. However, God can send specific dreams to communicate with us and to guide us as we ask Him. He can even send corrective dreams as nightmares, as with

God can send specific dreams to communicate with us and to guide us as we ask Him.

Abimelech (GENESIS 20:3) and Nebuchadnezzar (DANIEL 2). If you are in a situation where you have a tough time hearing from God, ask Him to send you a dream to make His guidance clear. You may be surprised at just how He shows up!

A "Good-for-You" Back Injury?

In the summer of 1972, a few of my good friends and I bought a 14-foot Hobie Cat catamaran. We loved the ocean and, at the time, I had given up surfing. A good day on Kailua Beach, one of the most beautiful beaches in the world, was like a day in heaven. If the day had 15- or 25-mile-per-hour winds, riding with one hull up in the air at a 45-degree angle (a.k.a. "hiking the Hobie Cat"), provided us the ultimate beach day. We didn't depend on waves (like surfing) and were not restricted by crowds. The entire ocean was our playground.

One day, we had good winds and I was the first one to take the catamaran out. However I had to beach the catamaran when I came back in, which required lifting it and pushing it up the sandy beach. In doing so, I injured my back. And that was essentially the end of my "hiking" days, as well as any running for that matter. I ended up going to the chiropractor once or twice a week for years. Whenever I saw people running, I would think of the "good old days" playing football, basketball, and surfing.

When you live with any injury or disability, you get used to it. My chiropractor told me that the worst thing for a bad back was a big stomach. "Imagine," he said, "how your back would feel if you had a bowling ball strapped to your stomach." I got the picture. It was the beginning of a keen awareness regarding my weight, eating habits, and what was needed to take care of my body: stretching and light weightlifting. He also told me that my body was like a building – it needed concrete and reinforcing steel bars for strength. My skeletal system was the steel bar structure and my muscles were the concrete. Both needed to be in balance.

But that was not the end of the lesson for me. A few years after becoming a Christian, what was a disability turned into a blessing. I started listening to Christian radio throughout the day, from the time I woke up, driving in my car, and as soon I got home. I exercised and stretched daily, both morning and evening. While exercising, I would listen to Christian messages and worship songs, and in that time I had many ideas. At first, I didn't react to these ideas. But they kept returning and eventually strong feelings rose up, creating a desire to take action. As I took action, I realized God was involved. I had stumbled on how He worked! He was guiding my steps by speaking to my heart through my mind.

> *He was guiding my steps by speaking to my heart through my mind.*

The Bible promises that God does speak to our hearts. In Ezra 1:1, God *"moved the heart of Cyrus...to make a proclamation..."* to allow the people to go back to Jerusalem and build the temple. Then He also moved the hearts of the people to return: *"Then the family heads...and the priests...everyone whose heart God had moved..."* (EZRA 1:5).

We see it again in 1 Samuel 10:9, *"As Saul turned to leave Samuel, God changed Saul's heart...."* In Daniel 1:9, *"God caused the official to show favor and sympathy to Daniel."* The prophet Nehemiah said, *"So my God put it into my heart to assemble the nobles, the officials and the common people for registration by families"* (NEHEMIAH 7:5).

Over the years, I was able to incorporate my time with God into most of my daily activities. I remember that Ray Comfort would say that he didn't just go shopping; he would witness at the mall, and while witnessing he would pick up whatever he needed. Now

I don't go to 24 Hour Fitness just to workout; I spend time with God and while listening to great bands and worshiping, I may as well work out.

When I clean the house, I think about the practical things God does, like recycling and purifying air and water, and while doing so I move my hands back and forth, so I may as well carry a vacuum hose! When I bathe the dog, I'll set aside time to worship God, turn on the warm water and bathe Mushu (our Japanese Spitz). Life is good with the right approach. God used my bad back to help me develop a good, disciplined program.

My New Friend, Jerry

Early in 1995, we hosted our First Assembly of God Life Group, a home Bible study. We had a group of about six to eight people that attended regularly. The group regularly started at 7 pm. One night, at about 7:30 pm, I was sitting alone at the dining table, and I thought no one was coming. Just then the doorbell rang. I wasn't sure if I was happy or sad. *Did I really want to have a study with only one person?* (Selfish me!) I opened the door only to greet someone I had never met before.

His name was Jerry Aldredge. We talked about family and history, and then discussed the Bible. Jerry is one of those guys you want around when you need a cheering squad. We started with a simple scripture: John 3:16, *"For God so loved the world that he gave his one and only Son, that whoever believes in him shall not perish but have eternal life."*

Normally, everyone knows this passage and it needs little explanation. Yet as we talked about what Jesus meant, Jerry was full of "Wows," "Oohs," and "Ahs." I felt like a seminary graduate explaining the most difficult Bible passage to someone who had never heard it before, with revelation coming from God.

Naturally, we connected. Jerry joined our group and eventually his wife, Ninia, came too. It was like adding sugar to a pie, our life group came alive. Jerry played the guitar and lead worship at the start of the study, ushering in the Holy Spirit.

God Moves Jerry On

So it was with great hesitation and apprehension when another life group formed in Aiea and I felt the Lord tell me to send Jerry and Ninia. My first impression was "No, Lord, not Jerry!" But over the next few weeks, I felt the Lord confirm His desire. I asked Jerry to pray about it. We believed the Lord would speak to Jerry. To the non-believer, this may sound like hocus pocus, but to the Christian, it is the foundation of our relationship with the one who first created wireless communication.

God confirmed that Jerry and Ninia were to leave and help launch another life group. Our last Bible study they attended was emotional. We were all sad. I wondered whether I really heard from God. But I believe it is better to take the action that He is guiding you towards rather than following your own feelings.

One good outcome was that my son Daven, who had just started playing guitar, took over leading worship. Jerry was God's instrument in helping Daven to grow in leading worship.

God Moves Me Too!

Jerry was gone from the group, but since we attended the same church, we were still connected. We had a shared desire to help those with substance addictions. Jerry had left the group almost eight months when God put him on my heart. I felt the Holy Spirit telling me that I should help Jerry financially. We had not talked about this at all, and I had not seen Jerry for months. Since I didn't know how much or when, I did nothing. The following month, January, I felt the Holy Spirit's prompting, but there was nothing definitive.

The week after the Superbowl, I felt the Holy Spirit say to give Jerry $1,000. So I went to the bank to get eight $100 bills and four $50s on Monday. By Friday I was sure the time had come, so I came home from work, went to my drawer, and pulled out the money. I thought for a second that the eight $100s were probably enough so I put them in an envelope and started walking out. When I got to the hallway just outside of my bedroom, I felt the Holy Spirit clearly say, "I told you $1,000." I stopped, turned around and retrieved the rest. I drove to Jerry's house, about three minutes away.

I handed him the envelope and said, "The Lord told me to give this to you." I later found out that in December, Jerry's brother needed to borrow money to rent an apartment. Ninia went to the automatic teller and withdrew $1,400 from their credit card account. Jerry's brother was to repay the money by the end of December. He never did. And with 18 percent credit card interest eating at them, they started nipping at each other. By the end of January, the nipping turned into marital problems. Finally, Jerry and Ninia decided to trust God and make peace. They ended their discussion with Ninia making the comment, "If we could get $1,000 back, we'll be fine!"

God heard them and blessed their trust in Him. I was blessed because I knew I had heard God via His wireless communication system.

8

God & Our Loved Ones

God Takes a Loved One ~ My Dad

My dad was the strongest, toughest, and smartest man I knew. He built the A-1 business from the ground up. He started as an electrician at the Pearl Harbor Shipyard then moved to private industry with AA Electric. In the 1950s he struck out on his own. He would go from house to house to ask if any electrical work was needed. "Do you need any lights in your bedroom?" he would ask, or, "Do you need *anything* repaired?"

Eventually he started bidding on electrical work for new houses and even small commercial work: retail stores and service stations. My uncle Yutaka was my dad's first helper and eventually he hired two more, then four. Soon he was running a shop of eight men. Then he moved to a location on School Street before finally landing at our current location in Mapunapuna.

Not only was my father tough emotionally, he was tough physically. He never got sick. He never had an operation, never went to the hospital, and never stayed home from work. Except once, the last time.

His only weakness was his love for his family. One day when I was about 10 years old, I was playing and told my friend Ronald to throw a wooden spear at another friend, Michael. I had trapped Michael and held him facing Ronald. To my horror Ronald threw the spear. Michael ducked and the spear pierced my mouth. I ran home, blood dripping down my mouth, shirt and pants. Dad rushed me to the hospital. While the doctors used gauzes and cotton swabs to clean the wound from dirt and germs, my dad fainted. He loved me.

Dad was a two-pack-a-day smoker. However, when the Surgeon General warned that smoking was a health hazard, my dad quit "cold turkey." He never struggled with quitting because he loved his family too much.

A Prayer Too Late?

It was a shock for our family when we learned that Dad, not yet 54 years old, had cancer of the colon. After they operated, we valiantly-yet-vainly believed that he would be okay. At this point we had no religious association or faith. Our secular thinking was if we kept believing, everything would be alright. It wasn't; my dad finally passed away.

A few years after becoming a Christian, I shared a prayer for my dad to my Heavenly Father: "Father, I hope that sometime in the past – maybe in a foxhole while he was in the war or at some time when a stranger shared the Gospel – I hope my dad came to know and trust in you!" My dad had already passed away and I realized that there was nothing that could be done about his eternity. He was gone.

A few years later, I discussed some of the evidence for the existence of God with my mom. She asked, "Why are you doing this?"

"So you can go to heaven," I answered.

She replied, "How do you know I'm not going to heaven?"

I said, "According to the Bible, the only way is to believe in Jesus."

She replied, "How do you know I don't believe?" Then she told me that when my father had been sick, they had gone together to church, hoping for healing and they had both became Christians.

In disbelief, I called my sister Sharon into my office and told her what Mom had said. She already knew about it.

"How come no one told me?" I said, shocked.

She responded, "Would it have made any difference?" I realized it wouldn't have. At that time, in late 1978, I was not yet a believer. But since I had become a believer, I was now in unbelievable joy. God had answered my hope before I had even hoped!

Sharon's Account: Last Days with Our Dad

Sharon later told us the story of Dad's last year. She was still living at home and was only 20 years old when Dad passed. This is her account:

"It was March 1978, the night before Dad's surgery, and I spent some time with Dad as he lay in his bed. He talked about his childhood... how he was the black sheep of the family. He referred to himself as the 'bad penny' that always kept popping up. I told him, 'You turned out the best! You should be proud of who you are now.' Dad was always a tough, strong man, but that night I saw a different side.

"Tears flowed freely from his eyes and I saw the vulnerable, human side of him. He asked me to turn off the light to hide the tears; he didn't want me to see him that way. I dimmed the lights and told him it was okay to cry. He said, 'I'm scared. I don't know what to expect from this surgery.'

"The day after his surgery, I picked up the phone and over-heard a conversation. My mom was talking to the doctor and he told her, 'The cancer has spread. He has three to six months left.' Mom responded: 'That's all?' I hurried downstairs to question my mom. She said Dad would be fine. I told her that I heard what the doctor had said on the phone, but she calmly replied, 'The doctor's wrong; Dad's going to be fine!' And for the next 10 months, Mom was extremely strong; she did it for our family.

"Mom kept talking to Dad about where they would travel when he got better, never about how sick he was. Every day she would tell him he was getting better. But one day I came home late in the afternoon and I overheard Mom sobbing in her bedroom, behind closed doors. I wasn't sure what to do. I wondered, *Should I go in and try to be strong for her? Or should I let her be?* I figured that she needed that time. I stood there silently with one hand on the doorknob; and my heart going out to her."

And without knowing it our Father was staying strong for us too.

"Daddy, Wait for Us in Heaven!"

In Dad's last month, he often spent hours sitting in a patio chair looking at the airplanes flying into the heavens. "I wonder where that plane is going?" he would ask. "I sure wish I could have been on that plane!"

The night Dad passed away, Mom stroked his forehead repeat-edly and told him, "Daddy, go with God. Go with God when you're ready. Go to heaven, build our new home and wait for us. We'll all come when it's our time. Wait for us, okay, Daddy?"

Dad worked at the shop until December 1978, literally until he died. He had provided until the end. In fact, he had set up enough work to last the business for an entire year after his death.

Ma Enokawa: "Guarantee She Went to Heaven!"

My wife Diana has a very loving family and they especially loved the matriarch of their family, Ma Enokawa. More than anyone else in all of God's creation, they loved Ma. And that love was built on the foundation of Ma's own love for her family.

Ma had a tough life. Her parents shipped her off to Japan to live with an aunt in Okinawa. She returned to her family in her mid-teens because she could work and provide income. During the Depression, life was especially hard for her pig-farming family. She worked as a live-in housemaid for another family.

At a young age, Ma married a boxer who turned out to be a gambler, too. He left her after their only child, Doris, contracted polio. Ma worked day and night to provide for her daughter. Eventually she saved enough to buy a small coffee shop on Nuʻuanu Avenue in downtown Honolulu.

Ma's second husband, Bert Enokawa, was born and raised on the island of Kauaʻi. He was also sent off to live with a well-to-do family in Okinawa. But when the war started, he returned to Honolulu. They met, married, and had their first child, Janice. Ma was forced to sell the coffee shop to raise her children.

Ma and Pop worked as cooks in the restaurant business for the rest of their lives. Ma worked in small restaurants and bars while Pop worked in the hotels. They were able to raise and support a family of seven, but due to long work hours they were rarely home to raise the kids. As a result, the children formed a close bond and this became the strength of the Enokawa family. Truth be told, fitting a family of seven into a four-bedroom house was no small miracle; it had a lot to do with the family's closeness.

Love's Finest Hour

Later in life, Ma contracted lung cancer and her eldest daughter Doris and her husband spared no expense to love and care for her. They eventually got a hospital bed for her and their living room became Ma's bedroom. Doris was crippled with polio from the age of three but was able to take care of her dying mother, 60 years later. They never even considered a nursing home or a hospice – it was simply out of the question. This was "love's finest hour."

My wife Diana was concerned about Ma's eternity so she invited Pastor Woodrow Yasuhara to come and share the Gospel. Ma believed that God existed; she even took her children to Salvation Army Church on Vineyard. She had done so much good in life; however, we knew doing good things was not enough to assure her place with God.

We knew doing good things was not enough to assure her place with God.

Pastor Yasuhara's gift was the ability to share Jesus in Japanese. He spoke in Japanese about what Jesus did on the cross. Ma received Jesus into her life that night. It was a good night for Diana and I as we drove Pastor Yasuhara home that evening. We had a peace knowing that Ma had solidified her relationship with Jesus.

A Beautiful Passing

The entire Enokawa family gathered at Doris' house the last weekend of February 1995. Ma began to experience discomfort and couldn't get out of bed. Her lung cancer had spread into her bones and our greatest fear for her was the excruciating pain. The only medication

Ma had was liquid Tylenol, of which she took very little. By Sunday night the pain worsened. By Monday she was taking regular doses of Tylenol. By that night, her pain was our pain for when Ma moved, she would utter a low groan: "*Oww, oww, oww!*"

Diana and I took off from work that day, and she stayed the night. She came home and we prayed: "Lord, if you are going to heal her, heal her. If you are going to take her, take her."

After Ma accepted Jesus as her Lord and Savior she attended the church's Japanese Service. Her favorite song was:

> "*Alleluia, Alleluia, Alleluia, Alleluia,*
> *Lord we love you,*
> *Lord we love you….*"

That morning, I sang her that favorite hymn continuously, in many different ways but kept the tune: *Jesus loves Ma, Ma loves Jesus, Jesus, Jesus, Thank you, Jesus.*

At about 8 am, I felt led to pray. At the time our son Jason, Diana's sister Elaine and Janice's husband Kenneth were with me at Ma's bedside. We joined hands and I thanked God for Ma and her life. I began to weep and couldn't stop. Time stood still. When I regained composure, I ended with the same prayer we had prayed earlier: "Lord, if you are going to heal her, heal her. If you are going to take her, take her."

The day before, Ma had struggled to open her eyes for even a second or two. When we ended the prayer, she opened her eyes wide, looked up, breathed twice, and then passed away peacefully. It was a beautiful passing.

Diana walked in a little later and realized her mom had passed on. She was happy and praised the Lord for allowing minimal suffering.

It wasn't until a few days later, as Diana walked our dogs down the hill where we live, that she was struck by the magnitude of the event. She later said, "I realized I would *never* be able to sit across Ma at the kitchen table, see her face and talk story with her. Only then did I truly realize the finality. I had a panic attack and found it hard to breathe."

Our son Jason told her, "Mom, guarantee Grandma went to heaven!"

Diana asked, "Jason, how do you know?"

Jason replied, "If you only saw her face." He recounted how just before Ma passed, she had a smile on her face as she looked up.

A Salmon Brings "Pop" Home

Bert "Pop" Enokawa worked hard all of his life, but he also played hard. He enjoyed drinking, social gambling, and laughing. He never learned to drive so his preferred mode of transportation was the bus. If there was a bus strike, Pop walked to work, nearly five miles each way. He worked in a hotel as a cook and his children cherished the goodies he brought home.

After Ma passed on and Pop retired, he was alone for many years. His children called a meeting and Janice volunteered to have him live with her family in Salt Lake. By the late '90s, Pop was having difficulty getting around. Each of the kids took a day to watch Pop, brought him breakfast and lunch, and took care of his needs. It was amazing to watch them arrive at a consensus about caring for Pop. It struck me that Christians could learn a lesson about caring for an aged parent from the Enokawa clan.

Diana's greatest concern for Pop was where he would spend eternity. One of the major obstacles in a Japanese family is the religious barrier. The words "God," "love," "heaven," "hell," and "eternity" have different cultural meanings. Whenever Diana raised the topic with Pop, she was met with a blank stare or disinterest. She became very concerned for her dad.

The Hook: A Fish Story

One day while we were driving near our church, First Assembly of God, I encouraged Diana to tell Pop the salmon story. The Pacific salmon spawns somewhere in the mountains above the Pacific Ocean. When they're ready, they travel downstream in a migratory pattern set from the beginning of time. As they reach maturity, they return to the freshwater stream of their origin to lay eggs.

One question that still puzzles scientists is how the salmon find their birthplace. Some of the salmon travel as far as 2,000 miles to return to the same little streambed from which they came – their "homeland."

Some scientists feel that if they can explain how the salmon return home, they can deny the idea of a Creator God. They seek a natural explanation. There is valid evidence that the salmon has senses that guide them. These sense the earth's magnetic field, the position of the sun, moon and stars, as well as the ability to detect the chemical composition of the fresh water from their birth. However, while these scientists use this to discredit God, they overlook one essential point: *Where did the salmon gain these senses? Could they have gained them from a Creator?*

Naturally, I believe God created the salmon and helps "guide" them home with an internal guidance system. This draws attention to the main issue: only God can bring the salmon home.

Why did God give the salmon such an intricate migratory system? And why are these same complex migratory habits also established for the Monarch butterfly, the sea turtle, and many different birds? Diana and I came to understand that God brings His creation home. Therefore, when we observe this miracle, we can understand that God wants to bring us home.

As we experience these feelings, the intention is that we would be drawn to God.

God gave us our own sensing system: a fear of death, emptiness, loneliness and guilt. As we experience these feelings, the intention is that we would be drawn to God. Diana recognized that her dad had an uncertain future as death was right around the corner.

The Final Hook

As we drove home, Diana mentioned that Pop had a really bad day. She feared he would not last the night. She sensed an urgency to again share the Gospel with him. So the next morning she returned to Janice's house and before she entered, she prayed, "Oh, God, don't let him be dead." She was relieved to find he was still alive.

Here's her story as she shared it with me in her own words:

"As I was bathing him, I shared the salmon story. Afterwards, we went into the living room where his favorite chair was situated. While rubbing cream and massaging his back, I told him how worried I was: 'I was so worried that you were going to die last night and I would come and find you dead this morning! I wouldn't have had a chance to tell you: "Thank you for raising us. I love you! You weren't the perfect father...but I know you did the best you could." If you died, Pop, do you know what would happen to you?'

"He said, 'I'm going home to heaven.'

"I told him, 'Pop, the only way you can go to heaven is if you believe in Jesus – that He died on the cross for your sins... And came alive after three days and went home to God in heaven.'

"I was still behind him, massaging his shoulders, when Pop started weeping. He said, 'I believe in Jesus.'

"And then I said, 'Pop we need to pray to ask Jesus to come into your heart and to forgive you of all of your sins. You need to really believe and trust in Jesus.' So we prayed.

"Pop had prayed what we call the 'Salvation Prayer' before, but this time I felt like he understood and was really sincere. I was at peace.

"Pop passed away later that year and his funeral was a joyous celebration."

9

God Partners in Our Business

One day, a competitor from the Big Island of Hawai'i called. JK Electric operates in Hilo, one of the rainiest cities in the United States. John Kimura was owner and president, and his company was the largest electrical contractor in Hilo. A $60-million construction project was coming up for bid and he wanted to know if we wanted to work together. John was a Christian and he knew I was one too, so he thought we would make a good team. However, our estimating team was extremely busy, so I politely declined.

A few weeks later, Dick Pacific Construction, one of the largest general contractors in the state, also called to inquire if we were bidding on the project. They were building the first phase of the new campus for Kamehameha Schools outside of Hilo. The next phase was priced in the millions of dollars. And, as a benefit, whoever won the second phase would be in position to negotiate the third phase. Phases two and three were worth twice as much as the first phase. Again I said we simply didn't have the time required to bid on the job. The bid date was only a week and a half away.

Afterwards, I prayed a simple prayer: "Father, are you telling me that we should bid on this?" The rest of the day it was on my mind and that night I felt the Holy Spirit guiding me to bid. The next day,

I gathered the estimating team and surveyed the projects we were already committed to bidding or servicing. We looked at which ones we could postpone and which we could decline. If we got our whole team working overtime, we could pull the estimate together in time. So we charged forward.

We ended up getting both projects. However, a major problem arose. The project included a large stadium with pole lights 90- to 150-feet high. The poles were supported by a huge concrete base that locked into the stadium. The supplier of the anchor bolts had furnished stainless steel bolts that did not meet contract specifications. How did they know? The bolts started rusting just before the project was completed.

God Uses Catastrophe

After a thorough investigation, the owner decided that we had to correct the situation. This meant removing the pole lights that were already installed, digging out the concrete pole base, and then reinstalling everything. It appeared to be a $1.5-million fix, not including the down time. Plus, no one could use the stadium during the repairs.

What do you do when you are faced with a catastrophe? Worry? Get angry? Look for someone to blame? Fire someone?

To a certain degree, our company was protected because the supplier was ultimately responsible. However, a problem is not resolved because another company is legally responsible. So after a month of going back and forth with the owner, one Saturday morning, an idea came to mind (which I know came from God).

I thought about finding a legal case to establish a precedent for the central issue: Could the owner force the supplier to change the pole bases if they didn't meet the contract specifications exactly

– even though they had met the practical essence of the contract specs? What if the incorrect anchor bolts would withstand the wind speed (105 mph) and last for the life of the installation (50 years), could the owners require the suppliers to spend $1.5 million for an upgrade that wouldn't gain much? I contacted my attorney to see if he could find a case that would help the supplier.

By Monday, my lawyer responded with such a case: the "Granite Case." Essentially, it protects subcontractors and suppliers from nuisance small suits whereby the supplier furnishes a material that meets all the relevant standards and codes, but is one quality below the owner's specification. The owner may require the supplier to give a fair credit for furnishing such material, but as long as it "works" for the situation, they cannot force a catastrophic correction that will hurt the supplier.

We presented the "Granite Case" to the architects. While we supported them, if we forced the correction, the supplier would probably sue us all for damages. And with the law in their favor, we would probably lose. The owner was not happy with the situation, but they realized the alternative was worse. Ultimately, a "fix" to the existing system was made. It was very clear to my project manager and me that God was guiding the solution and giving favor on the other side of the table. The passage rang more and more true: *"All we have accomplished you have done for us"* (ISAIAH 26:12).

"All we have accomplished you have done for us" (ISAIAH 26:12).

Does God Bring People to Your Business?

Author Peter Drucker shared his business philosophy in his book, *Management: Tasks, Responsibilities, Practices.* One of the key tenets of faith he presented is that people are our greatest assets. And looking back on decades of business, I recognize that God had a hand in bringing leaders and workers to A-1. Just as the Lord brought the mighty men to King David so he could accomplish God's plan, so God provided for our company, too.

God provided for our company, too

When I get to heaven, I'll ask Jesus how he brought so many leaders to A-1. Meanwhile, I want to share a few examples that stand out. This does not imply added importance to people mentioned or a lack of importance to those that are not. I am merely sharing a few that clearly show God's divine hand.

Art the Apprentice

Art Aoki worked all of his life for one of our competitors: Halfhill Electric. When Halfhill closed its doors, I received a call from a union representative. Now, I had not initiated the call, nor was I looking for good men; further more I didn't know any of Halfhill's men. The union rep told Art to contact me, so I laid out our business philosophy for him. I wasn't trying to sweet talk him, nor did I make any special offers. While other shops were enticing him with offers of immediate promotion to foreman, I told Art I couldn't promise him anything. He would have to start as a regular journeyman, but he could climb as high as he wanted to go from there.

Art joined A-1 and immediately started his meteoric rise through the ranks of our company. Probably his toughest challenge was agreeing to work under one of our old-timers, Charley Toyama, on the Honolulu Park Place project. I told Art he had an opportunity to learn the A-1 system from Charley. However, it was a big step down from being general foreman at Halfhill Electric where he had supervised the whole shop.

Since then, Art has been in charge of some our largest projects: the Waikiki Landmark, the State Capital renovation, the University of Hawai'i Medical Center (John Burns School of Medicine), and the recently completed Outrigger Beachwalk. Art is a blessing from the Lord Himself.

Cory Saw God's Guiding Hand

Another great story comes in a young man named Cory Young. He came to the United States in the early '80s. He graduated in 1990 from the University of Hawai'i with a bachelor of science in electrical engineering and went to San Diego to look for work. The economy wasn't doing great and on August 2, 1990 Iraq invaded Kuwait. Five days later the United States started a build-up for Operation Desert Storm. That invasion took place in January 1991. The uncertainties that war created didn't make for good business expansion plans. It was not the best time to look for work, but for this young Chinese college graduate, it was the God's time.

Cory's mom lived in Honolulu and a neighbor named Mr. Yamada gave her an ad for an entry-level electrical engineer he had seen in the local paper. She sent it to Cory and he promptly submitted his application to A-1.

When we got his application we saw that he lived in San Diego. We filed it away as we were not interested in bringing in someone from the mainland.

Meantime, Cory continued to have a tough time finding a job in San Diego, so he contacted a friend working for the Japan Travel Bureau who offered him a part-time job in Honolulu. Cory prayed to God for help in finding a solid full-time job. He made an unusual (he called it "shameful") request to God: "If I find a job before year's end (1990), I will recognize You are the provider. If the job is found after 1990, then it will be my own doing." (Cory has grown much since that early prayer.)

When Cory returned to Hawai'i, he remembered that he had sent a resume to an electrical company, but he couldn't remember which one. He checked with his mom, knowing that she never threw anything away. Indeed, she had kept the ad and Cory called Sharon who then brought his application to me. She explained that the guy we thought was in San Diego actually lived here and would like an interview. We interviewed Cory on November 19 and hired him on December 19, 1990.

Cory recognized God's hand. Although I didn't know God back then, we recognize the blessing Cory has been as one of our estimators, for what is now almost 20 years.

Carl: God's Ace

Hygrade Electric was one of the largest electrical contractors in the state in the early '90s and they completed many of Hawai'i's hotels and large projects. As things happen in our industry, Hygrade closed its doors as its owner moved on in life.

The closure turned out to be an opportunity for us, as one of their main foremen left after completing his projects. His name was Carl Matsubara. A friend and Christian brother of mine came in one day and said, "Did you know Carl Matsubara is leaving Hygrade?" I asked, "Who's Carl Matsubara?"

It turned out that Carl was one of the industry's top foremen. He had directly supervised many of the largest projects in Hawai'i over the past 20 years – from the Hyatt Regncy Waikoloa on the Big Island, the Grand Hyatt Wailea on Maui, and the 'Ihilani Hotel on

O'ahu. He was so loyal that as Hygrade started layoffs, many had abandoned the sinking ship, but not Carl. He remained loyal to the very end. He simply would not abandon the company in order to secure a better position with another company.

My friend asked if I wanted to meet Carl and I answered, "I would be if he was interested in meeting and talking to me after he left Hygrade."

A Surprising Guy

My friend called a few days later and told me that Carl was open to meeting with me. From my friend's descriptions I had certain expectations of a James Bond-type person, but when we met, I was surprised! Carl was regular Japanese guy. In fact, if you saw Carl on the street you wouldn't even think he was in construction.

We spent the first half hour getting to know each other. The thing I remember was much laughter. Then I shared the philosophy of A-1. I also shared our current program where we set aside a portion of our net worth to invest back into our greatest assets, our people. In other words, we didn't mind losing money to keep our people over the long run. "The Yamadas are like farmers," I told Carl, "and when it doesn't rain, a farmer doesn't close up, sell the land, and slaughter the cattle. We're all in for the company and the men."

Carl came to work for A-1. God's hand was all over this situation. We didn't chase after Carl; we didn't even know who he was! And when we did find out, we didn't try to entice him. Yet he came.

God's hand was all over this situation.

The key was that he was one of the most humble guys I had ever met. And that character trait, paired with his obvious talent, is precious in a leader.

It is not possible to list all the detailed accomplishments that would allow you a glimpse of the tremendous impact God made on A-1 through Carl. And, by listing such accomplishments, I would be not giving proper credit to others at A-1, that God also brought and used to have a major impact as well.

The essence is to present a strong and simple case that shows what I know: God brought the major players to A-1.

School of Medicine: Attack!

Diana and I both graduated from the University of Hawai'i (UH). Our three children also attended UH, so the university holds a special place in our hearts. A-1 has done a number of major projects at UH, including the Pacific Ocean Science and Technology (POST) Building and the Agricultural Building. However, the gem of the decade for construction was to be its Medical School. Budgeted at $115 million, it was a highly desirable project, but not just for obvious reasons. It would push A-1 to the forefront of "design-assist" projects we had defined as our future market.

The challenge: our chief competitor had already secured the project.

Wasa Electrical had already been working on the project for almost a year. They had participated in the preconstruction meetings that help the owners, architect, and engineers decide the method of construction and the scope of the project. They also worked to resolve construction issues and solve coordination issues that could add unnecessary costs to the project. Wasa's rep also made trips to the continental U.S. to see the specialized lab equipment needed for the project. Everything was in Wasa's favor.

Impossibly Possible?

In mid-December 2002, A-1 received what we call a 100 percent Design Development (DD) plan from Hawaiian Dredging and Construction. It is a formal request for subcontractors to bid, but because of the tight two-week period to submit the bid, I thought it was just another round of budget pricing. There was no way it would be used to select a final electrical contractor. In addition, because we were pricing a number of other projects, we were in no rush to price this one with any degree of seriousness.

On December 17, 2002, my lead estimator for the project, Glenn, asked me how to approach the project. We had been using costs from other jobs to price the project. I told him to keep the same budget as he didn't have the time to do a complete pricing and it was due by December 30.

I felt a nudge (which I later recognized as God) to check if the contractor and owner, Hawaiian Dredging and Construction (HDC), might select the electrical subcontractor from this level of pricing. So I asked Glenn to check with HDC. He came back and said that indeed it may lead to selecting a subcontractor because HDC wanted them involved in the preconstruction process. One can never be sure if what the general contractor says will dictate as there are many other circumstances beyond their control.

At that point I felt God tell me to charge forward on the project. I gathered the estimating team – five estimators/foreman and one design engineer – and we spent the next two weeks doing a complete estimate. On January 3, 2003 we turned in our price to HDC – in record time – a major undertaking considering the size of the project.

What happened next amazed us.

Late in the afternoon of January 7, HDC called: A-1 was selected as the contractor for the UH Medical School. I saw God's hand in the process:

1. The gentle nudge that I received from Him to check about the selection.

2. HDC allowed us three additional days to complete our price.

3. Due to the Christmas season, we were able to delay pricing on other projects. If this project had come a month later, I would not have been able to pull our team off for two weeks.

4. God gave the team wisdom to recognize incomplete areas and electrical systems and price them correctly, enabling us to secure the project.

5. God gave us favor in the timing of the subcontractor selection so we could properly "attack" the project. HDC wanted to make a quick selection. Had we not had the right information, we would not have been selected because our initial budgets were much higher than our final price.

The project started off a bit rocky, but within three months, the team that HDC had assembled gelled and the project became one of the smoothest A-1 has ever been involved in. I believe God gave favor to that team.

God Gives "Buy-&-Sell" Signals

As part of our corporate global plan, A-1 hedges our business via financial instruments. Basically, the hedge works like this in theory: If the stock market falls apart, the economy will turn down, experience a recession and inevitably construction will be bad. The hedge helps protect our business on the down side.

One part of the hedge is that we are buyers of gold and sellers of the stock market. (Please refer to the three charts: SPX and Gold in the Photo Gallery section.) Gold is a hedge against a drastic collapse in the dollar which would negatively impact construction. As sellers of the stock market, we sell the S&P 500 index in a way to hedge against a recession which would negatively impact our construction market. These are not pure hedges as they do not offer perfect protection. Our bonding company guarantees A-1 will complete a project. Our banks go a bit "crazy" over our use of financial instruments. As long as everything is kept in balance, the idea is sound, so they both allow us to execute our plan.

In 2001, we sold short S&P futures contracts and (we profited when the S&P 500 fell) in significant amounts. After the September 11 terrorist attacks, these increased in value tremendously. By summer 2002, our hedge portfolio had increased steadily, and the S&P 500 was nearing the 850 level. We started closing out our positions and closed most of them between S&P 500 levels 850 and 820. The S&P 500 briefly dropped below 800 then quickly rallied to 960. We then re-established new positions between 920 thru 950 at which point the index fell in late 2002 back below the 800 level. It rallied to near the 950 level and then had a slow descent to the 800 level. It was like a roller coaster. The key principle to understand here is that A-1 had a substantial portfolio that would help to protect us in the event of a serious recession.

On March 20, 2003 the United States attacked Iraq under the code name "Operation Iraqi Freedom." Gloom and doom set in as many were glued to their televisions watching the bombings and the new war. Oil wells burned out of control. We were shocked at the increasing price of oil. Between November 2002 and March 2003 the price soared from $25 per barrel to $38 per barrel. I was surprised because after the attack in March 2003, the S&P 500 index hit bottom, below 800 then began a steady climb through April and to hit 920. It then fell back to 890 on April 27, 2003.

My struggle was what to do with our portfolio. Remember, if the S&P 500 index went up, my portfolio lost value. In theory that is fine since if it continues to rise and the economy gets better, construction in Hawai'i should be fine. However, you never really know. Therein lay my struggle: As long as the index was rising would all be well? Or should I close out my hedge? I was constantly in prayer, "Father, what should I do?"

On April 27, the Lord answered. I had a dream that I was buying the S&P 500 index. I was confused. Normally my program is not to buy, but simply to hedge when necessary. After 9-11, a continual hedge seemed necessary. But not in my dream.

I realized God had given me a "buy signal." I was to close out my hedge! By April 28, I effectively closed out and turned everything into cash. As it turned out, the SPX at 800 was the low for that cycle. God knows all things and had given me the direction I needed.

Dreams of Gold

I've always been fascinated with gold. We have gold rings, gold chains, and gold accessories. The Bible even talks about gold over 400 times!

One of Diana's favorite actors was Sean Connery and I liked to think I was like him. I even signed Diana's yearbook with the code name "007," his title character as James Bond. It just so happens that one of Sean Connery's Bond movies included lots and lots of gold. "Goldfinger" was arguably the best Bond movie ever. Well, at least for Diana and me!

In my early years I lost quite a bit of money chasing after "pie in the sky" gold dreams. When you're young it doesn't matter, you can always make it back and there'll always be another investment. Things have changed. As Father Time marched on, I came to understand that people depend on my moves in our business. The future is now. Our business capital needs protection. On a small net worth, we currently provide for about 160 employees. So our hedge portfolio is our insurance package against catastrophe.

Our gold hedge program started in late 2002, and picked up steam during 2003 after we closed out our S&P futures contracts. In a futures contract, each gold contract is for 100 ounces of gold. If gold is selling at $600/ounce, the value of one contract is $60,000, for which the margin (amount of investment you need to commit towards the purchase) might be $2,500 however it varies. The leverage is tremendous. With a total margin investment of $100,000, you might control $2,400,000 worth of gold. If gold goes up by 10 percent from $600/ounce to $660/ounce, you've made $240,000. Of course if gold goes down five percent, you are wiped out. And, long before that, you also owe money to your brokerage, and it may be money you don't have. So it was understandable that our gold buying made our bonding company and our bankers a little nervous.

A-1 protected itself in two ways: first, we did not allow our portfolio to get heavily leveraged. And second, we placed sell stop orders relatively close to the latest price of gold. If gold falls, you're automatically stopped out. Of course, this creates a lot of quick protective sales as gold bounces around, but you are never exposed to a big fall, and have the benefit of a good gain as gold moves upward. Again, this is a simplistic explanation. If your trading education is coming from this book, you don't belong in the futures market. In fact, if you're scratching your head over this, keep your day job.

This leads to the point of this part of my life, another dream. Gold had just risen past $400, reached $432/ounce, and fell back to $415/ounce. On April 5, 2004, I had a dream from God that gold would fall by $60/ounce.

I told this to my family, including my nephew Craig who works at A-1 as a project engineer. Craig graduated with an economics degree and was interested in investments. He quickly got interested in gold and other natural resources – mineral-type investments. When I first had the dream, I wasn't sure if it was really going to happen. If I was sure, I would have to close out all my long positions and go "short gold."

Soon after, gold steadily fell. Immediately my sell stops closed out my positions and any new ones established were very small ones. Gold fell below $400, then below $390. As it fell Craig and I were watching, not to make money but to see if the dream was from God. Only He could truly know what was going to happen. I was satisfied to know that He forewarned me about the future, even though I didn't profit from the dream. It was all about a relationship with Him.

It was all about a relationship with Him.

Then gold bounced around in the $380 to $390 zone for a while, finally falling below $380 and one day touched $372. God was revealing something special. Gold had fallen by exactly $60/ounce, as God had revealed in my dream. The only problem was I wasn't sure if it could keep falling, so I didn't take advantage of it though I did start re-establishing our gold positions at the $380-390 level.

That was the bottom for the cycle and gold began it climb to the current $900 level as this is written.

I must truthfully state at this point in our hedge (early 2007), the stock market has gone almost straight up since early 2003, and although gold has done well, the hedge portfolio has not done well at all. However, I am pleased. If we made a lot of money on the hedge it would have meant a weak stock market and possibly a weak construction market. I'd rather do well in construction as that is the business the hedge is intended to protect.

I am not writing this to boast that God has given me some supernatural wisdom or knowledge to trade the markets. He has not. This is written so that you may know that our God can communicate with us when He chooses. It's up to us to have our receivers tuned in to His channel.

God can communicate with us when He chooses. It's up to us to have our receivers tuned in to His channel.

10

What Is It About God's Power?

As I look back on my very short walk with God, I am amazed and humbled to think that He could use a little Japanese guy – all of five-feet and five inches (and shrinking!) – to do some of the things He wanted done. I was never good in sports. I had to study diligently to get three Bs and an A in school. I had a difficult time with engineering classes and when I finally graduated, I thought, *What do I actually know? What can I do as an electrical engineer?* Nothing came to mind and I remember a touch of fear running through me.

In the early '70s, when I had finally gained a little confidence I made some poor investments. I lost such a huge amount of money that I was still writing off the losses in the '90s. And when I turned my full attention to our electrical business I almost bankrupted it. I credit my wife Diana for standing with me as many of today's postmodern women would have crucified their husbands, take the money and run.

My Greatest Struggle

As I started observing God's voice and hand in our lives, the biggest struggle was my pride. When God moved, and something beyond the natural and logical took place, it seemed impossible for me to not take at least a little credit. In construction, hundreds of problems would come up and I would always solve them. I thought I was brilliant.

When the A-1 portfolio increased, my first tendency was to think I was a master financier. I remember analyzing the A-1 positions as they grew leaps and bounds and thinking that I shouldn't have to wash dishes or clean the bathrooms. My time was too valuable for such mundane chores! Maybe I should talk to Diana and hire a maid. I didn't, but it did cross my mind.

Within weeks of having these thoughts, the portfolio started to crash and that quickly jarred me back to reality. I wasn't great; I wasn't even good! I was an average Joe that our creator had chosen to do some of His work.

> *"If my people, who are called by my name, will humble themselves and pray and seek my face and turn from their wicked ways, then will I hear from heaven and will forgive their sin and will heal their land."* (2 CHRONICLES 7:14)

God was healing my land, my business, and my family. I wasn't doing anything. Since I've realized this truth in the last few years, my life has become easier. God is living and active in our lives and wants to impact our world. He's looking for people willing to partner with Him so He can work through them. With this understanding, it has been easier to recognize that He is the One doing the work.

He's looking for people willing to partner with Him so He can work through them.

Isaiah 26:12 says, "All that we have accomplished you have done for us."

It isn't my ability that God is concerned with, but my relationship with Him. It's about deepening and growing as I allow Him to work in my business and life. Yes, we can ask Him to be a part of the things we do. However, why should He show up if the motivation of our heart is simply to look good? It's more likely that He will use someone else to accomplish His purposes. Acknowledge His accomplishments quickly; it will make life easier and so much better!

What's the Greatest Work of God?

God's supernatural power has a purpose: that we may know His love. Father God sent his son Jesus and allowed Him to perform miracles so that we would know He had been sent by the Father. Further, God raised Jesus from the dead so we would all know God (JOHN 3:16). And through that eternal sacrifice, God offers His forgiveness for all of us to receive as we believe (ACTS 2:22-24, 37-38).

> *God's supernatural power has a purpose: That we may know his love.*

However, miracles are not the point.

On the contrary, the miraculous is only a *means* for God to achieve His ultimate objective. They help us to know that God crosses over from His spirit world into ours and interacts with us. Christians are unaffected by His supernatural because they don't believe that He can and does work miracles today. Others are overly focused on chasing after His power.

Neither is correct.

Jesus gives us a clear picture of this: At the Last Supper He told His disciples to trust in Him. He then talks about heaven, telling us that *He is the way to heaven.* Philip asked for more evidence, saying, *"Show us the Father."*

Jesus answered, *"Don't you believe that I am in the Father, and that the Father is in me?"* (JOHN 14:10) Then He said, *"...at least believe on the evidence of the miracles themselves."* (JOHN 14:11)

Jesus continued on to say, "*Anyone who has faith in me will do what I have been doing. He will do even greater things than these....*" The word "*these*" refers to the miracles Jesus performed that validate that the Father is in Jesus. And the "*greater things*" are the people coming to Christ to become children of God.

God's ultimate purpose is the salvation of our souls. So although the spiritual gifts are active and wonderful (1 CORINTHIANS 12), they are not the goal. For example, if someone is healed of disease but his soul is not born-again, he will die and spend eternity separated from God. Once a person trusts in God and is "saved" through Jesus, he enters into an eternal relationship with the Father.

The Ultimate Gift

The spiritual gifts listed in 1 Corinthians 12:7-11 include wisdom, knowledge, faith, healing, miraculous powers, prophecy, distinguishing between spirits, tongues, and interpretation of tongues. Love is not listed as a gift, but I believe it may be the ultimate gift given by the Holy Spirit.

At the end of 1 Corinthians, Paul also lists three categories of gifts:

1.   *Gifts of People's Roles*: Apostles, prophets, and teachers
     (1 CORINTHIANS 12:28, EPHESIANS 4:11)

2.   *Motivational Gifts*: Helps and administrations
     (1 CORINTHIANS 12:28, ROMANS 12:6-8)

3.   *Spiritual Gifts*: Miracles, healing and tongues
     (1 CORINTHIANS 12)

Paul concludes: "*Are all apostles? Are all prophets? Are all teachers? Do all work miracles? Do all have gifts of healing: Do all speak in tongues? Do all interpret?"* The obvious answer is no. He then drives to this main point: *"But eagerly desire the greater gifts,"* (1 CORINTHIANS 12:31) and the greatest gift is love.

What follows then in the Scripture is a long lesson on the ineffectiveness of various types of works without love (1 CORINTHIANS 13:1-3). Finally, Paul concludes: *"And now these three remain: faith, hope, and love. But the greatest of these is love"* (1 CORINTHIANS 13:13).

Though most agree that the greatest is love, not all agree how we might attain this love. For most of my Christian years, I believed that even if I was upset, I could react with (*agape*) love and be patient and kind. I thought I was walking in the Spirit and could react in love even in distress. But simply reacting in love is not what Jesus wants for our lives. I believe Jesus wants us to have His unconditional love for people that we cannot love. Can we have agape for a brother that has hurt us for 20 years? Can I love someone who cuts me off on the freeway, putting my life and the lives of my family at risk? Can I?

The ultimate supernatural work of salvation and sanctification is to love as Jesus loved. Therefore, we should pray for Jesus' agape love for those who are tough to love. It's no different than praying for a miracle. Previously, I had rarely prayed to agape my enemies, my "unlovables." Even if I did, I did not pray for it consistently and persistently.

> *The ultimate supernatural work of salvation and sanctification is to love as Jesus loved.*

Jesus said much about unconditional agape love:

1. At the Last Supper, He told His disciples: *"Love one another. As I have loved you, so you must love one another."* (JOHN 13:34).

2. On the mountainside, Jesus instructed: *"Love your enemies..."* (MATTHEW 5:44).

3. Jesus also taught his disciples to *"always pray and not give up"* (LUKE 18:1).

Unlocking Agape in Our Hearts

In this book, while I have shared much about seeing God's supernatural hand in my life, I realize that seeing Him move is really not just about the miraculous. It's about love; growing in my love for Him. And, as a result, letting that love overflow into my relationship with others: my wife, my mom, my kids, my fellow workers, and even those people I don't care for. Yet the agape love that God wants us to have comes only from Him.

God can give us unconditional agape love as easily as He can heal someone of cancer or raise another from the dead. Two passages show us how to unlock agape love for ourselves.

The first is found in Romans 5:3-5: *"Not only so, but we also rejoice in our sufferings, because we know that suffering produces perseverance; perseverance, character; and character, hope. And hope does not disappoint us, because God has poured out His love into our hearts by the Holy Spirit, whom He has given us."*

I believe when we are gentle and kind to someone who is an irritant to us in our daily lives, we endure suffering as we *"deny ourselves"* the pleasure of striking back, as Jesus' commanded in Mark 8:34. God is pleased as we grow in perseverance, character, and hope. Ultimately God reacts by pouring out His love into us.

The second Scripture to help unlock agape is found in Matthew 7:7-8, *"Ask and it will be given to you... for everyone who asks receives...."* As we pray for agape love, God answers in His time. We will receive a supernatural love that surpasses the mind. However, our part is that we must continue to *"pray and not give up!"* The problem is that few Christians really want to love the unlovables. They can be gentle and kind, but rejoice in harboring a secret grudge in their souls. Some, thankfully very few, even think that praying for this seemingly impossible agape love is "foolish."

When the body of Christ starts to sincerely pray and not give up until "God determines," then it is the right time for the outpouring of the Holy Spirit. He will pour love into our hearts. That's when revival will start.

Until then, we as the body will struggle along, hoping for a glimpse of His supernatural power to show up in our lives now and then. Then, when the supernatural happens once in a blue moon, we will hang on to such isolated events and tell stories about how our great God showed up in our lives "once upon a time."

We pray too much for revival to come.

We should be praying for God's agape love to come into our hearts for those for whom Jesus died.